LaGuardia's Fire Chief

The Story of Patrick Walsh,
an Irish-American Fire Chief

Kathleen Walsh Packard

Fire Buff House Publishers

New Albany, Indiana

FRONTISPIECE: Patrick Walsh and Mayor Fiorello LaGuardia assess the state of a fire. The two competed to see who could arrive first at fires.

Library of Congress Cataloging in Publication Data
Packard, Kathleen Walsh

LaGuardia's Fire Chief
Library of Congress Catalog Number: 92-71338
ISBN 0-925165-11-5

Originally published by Gateway Press, Inc. in 1992 under the title, "Fling Old Glory." This new edition includes the complete original text and pictures as well as additional pictures.

Any statements made herein or any references to any persons real or imaginary are those of the author and not of the publisher. Books and articles quoted or cited in the text under the usual fair use allowances are acknowledged in the notes.

Published by Fire Buff House, Division of Conway Enterprises, Inc.
P.O. Box 711, New Albany, Indiana 47151
© Kathleen Walsh Packard, 1993

Book design by Dolores Elise Brien
Cover design by Ron Grunder
Graphic revisions for this edition by Pam Jones

Printed in the United States of America

LaGuardia's Fire Chief

To my brother Jack

Contents

Preface

To us who found asylum here,
Is dear Old Glory doubly dear;
And swear again, we do,
That fatherland or motherland
Between us now no more can stand
We owe our all to you.

After my mother died in Brooklyn in 1979 at age eighty-five, I helped my sister sort out Mother's belongings and decide what should be passed on to her children or grandchildren. Since space was limited in her apartment, Mother had the habit of storing odds and ends in suitcases under her bed. The contents of these turned out to be mostly newspaper clippings from the 1930's and 1940's. Some were pasted on drawing paper; the rest, yellowing and fragile, had been tossed in the suitcases in no particular order.

I remembered that I had mulled over these clippings from time to time while growing up in our house in Flatbush. They were about my grandfather, Patrick Walsh, who had been the New York City Fire Commissioner under Mayor LaGuardia in the 1940's, and about my father, Michael F. Walsh, who had been Secretary of State in New York and, following that, a State Supreme Court Justice.

I stood in my mother's bedroom wondering what we should do with all this and who in the family would appreciate such a collection. It then occurred to me that likely no one would and that these clippings probably would wind up in someone else's suitcase to grow more yellow and unreadable with each passing year. The thought of that happening filled me with a deep sadness.

At that moment it occurred to me that I could do something about it; I could pass on their story, knowing that if I didn't it perhaps would be lost forever.

Most people's stories are, indeed, lost forever. We know nothing of countless rich human lives because these individuals were not subjects for history and no loved one ever wrote about them. It seemed to me that, although my grandfather and father were not subjects of history in the usual sense, they were, in their own way, representative of immigrant family history in the early twentieth century and particularly reflected the Irish experience in New York City. I decided to tell their story against this background.

With the suitcase still open on my mother's bed, I committed myself to begin working on a book when I retired from my civil service job with New York State. This feeling of commitment not only lingered in me but it increased so that, a year and a half later, I decided to go on a half-time schedule at work and use the other half of my time to start my research.

On a drizzly day in September, 1981, I took the Long Island Rail Road into Flatbush and the subway to Brooklyn Heights to walk the streets that Patrick Walsh walked during fifty-five years. The houses the family lived in were still standing. The parish church they frequented seemed hardly touched by time.

In the following months I took many trips to Lower Manhattan, spending hours in places like the Municipal Research Library and the LaGuardia archives in the old City Hall Courthouse. I hounded Uncle Paul, Patrick's only living son, trying in every way to jog his memory of his father.

I discovered very soon, however, that my new project was not quite like the research I had been accustomed to in graduate school assignments. The material touched me too closely. I had been thirteen when my grandfather died and I remembered him very well. While on one level I clearly admired him, there was another level on which I resented him.

Grandpa was of the "old school," idealistic and competitive at the same time, and always the strict disciplinarian. Although his coming to America at age nineteen was a rebellion against his father, he expected only obedience in his own household. My own father, though a softer personality, embodied Patrick's values. Reverence for authority and the drive to achieve or excel within a worthy career were handed down, through Michael, to my generation of five Walsh grandchildren. I resented the burden and questioned the values which, in my view, chose principle over the human person. I found their world view too black and white, insufficiently tolerant of the gray areas of life.

But researching Grandpa's biography brought me into contact with the other redeeming facets of his personality. He loved his family intensely and suffered through the loss of four young ones. He liked to read poetry and wrote his own, which while sentimental was always heartfelt. He had an affinity for nature and the outdoors, and considered a ten-mile walk with one of his sons an afternoon's recreation.

In a broader spectrum Patrick Walsh was a prime example of the Irish immigrant's devotion to the Catholic church. He perhaps went farther than many in making the Catholic religion the central inspiration and commitment of his life. Also, like numerous other Irish immigrants before and after him, he became a fervent American patriot. Scholars have pointed to the tendency of the Irish who, while insisting on their own parochial school system in a largely Protestant society, felt compelled to prove that they were, nonetheless, one hundred percent American. In fact, many Irish Catholics gradually saw themselves in the role of defender of the country's morality against the forces of decay from within and without.

Patrick's life was typical of a group and yet singularly his own. The human details that are the stuff of a life are what fascinate because it is in the detail, and not the generalization, that we find our own lives. From the very limited sources that exist, I have tried to recapture his personality and how he raised his family and pursued a career in his adopted country.

Kathleen Walsh Packard
Samish Island, Washington
December, 1991

Prologue

The New York City Fire Department's Special Order No. 166 for September 23, 1946, read as follows:

> It is with profound and sincere regret that announcement is made of the death of retired Fire Commissioner and Chief of Department Patrick Walsh which occurred at 5:30 A.M. September 21, 1946.
>
> . . . The funeral escort shall consist of a Regiment of three Battalions, four companies each (twenty-four men to a company).
>
> . . . 6 Deputy Chiefs shall be pallbearers
>
> . . . The Members of the Department Band shall be directed to report in uniform at State and Hicks Street at 9 A.M.
>
> . . . White gloves to be worn. . . .

The narrow streets of old Brooklyn Heights were ill-suited to contain the crowd that gathered at St. Charles Borromeo Church on Sidney Place: the formal assemblage of uniformed firemen, the Dominican clergy in their black and white robes, the two-by-two-file of relatives, the New York City officials, the friends from both public and private life, and the merely curious. The funeral cortege had taken an intentional detour in order to pass the nearest firehouse, Engine 224 on Hicks Street. The firemen in formation at the entrance raised their arms in stiff salute.

For those who managed to cross the threshold of the turn-of-the-century immigrant gothic church, the trumpet blasts from the Fire Department Band were gradually drowned out by the solemn strains of the church organ. Two of the three priests meeting the funeral procession at the altar rail were Jack and Paul, the Dominican sons of Patrick Walsh. The Bishop of Brooklyn, Thomas E. Molloy, sat in the episcopal throne above the rows of clergy filling the altar sanctuary. Patrick's second wife Annie, his sons Michael and Joseph, their wives and Michael's five children, filled the front pews.

More than the rich ceremony of the Funeral Mass, the profusive eulogies, the pageantry of robes and uniforms, music and incense, it was the church itself that recalled the presence of the man to those who knew him intimately. Patrick and Mary Ann had been married there in 1892. The church register records the baptismal dates of their children, and five sons had been altar boys at church services. Although the family had moved from house to house, they were always within walking distance of this red brick structure where Patrick attended daily mass. From the May afternoon in 1935, when Mary Ann dropped dead in the main aisle, Patrick attended two daily masses, one in her memory. In 1938 he had remarried before the same altar. The funeral mass this day was a final visit home.

Walsh Ancestry

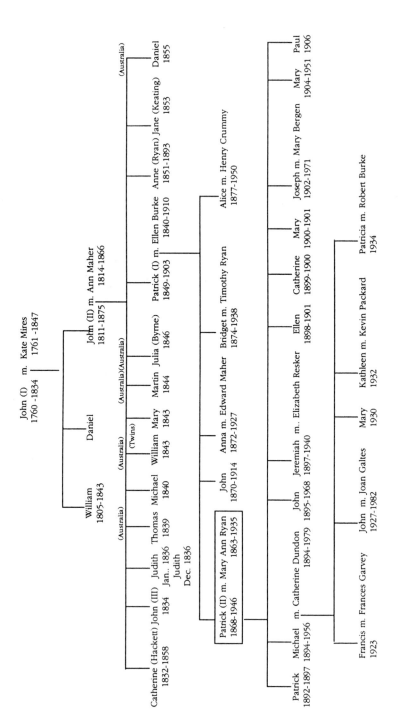

CHAPTER ONE

The View from Ballydine
1868 - 1888

The first Irish ancestor anyone remembered was John Walsh, Patrick's great-grandfather, born in 1760 and deceased in 1834. Patrick had it, by family lore, that this original John (who was to complicate all storytelling by propagating a John who propagated a John) had moved to County Tipperary from County Waterford where it was reputed that he owned an estate of 500 acres. Such wealth resting in Catholic hands in late eighteenth century Ireland is astounding. But family lore must often bow to historical scrutiny. It could well be true that a Walsh ancestor moved from Waterford to Tipperary but the likelihood is that this happened a hundred years earlier, in late seventeenth century.

The challenge to the traditional story lies in a graveyard. John Walsh and his wife Kate Mires are buried near the wall of Cormac's chapel on the Rock of Cashel, a well known tourist site rich with Irish history, four miles from the Walsh farm in Ardmayle. A County Tipperary historian asserts that a migrant from Waterford could not have immediately claimed a burial place on the Rock of Cashel. It was not that simple. Burial rights on the Rock are rooted much further back than the early 1800's.[1] The Walshes probably lived in the Cashel area a century earlier. A church report in 1760 names two Walshes in Ardmayle, Simon and James, most likely brothers. Perhaps one of the two was John Walsh's father.

John and Kate might have had a sizeable family but the only record is of three children born when their parents were close to fifty years of age—William in 1805, Daniel, date unknown, and John in 1811. The dates of the parents' lives are etched, seemingly forever, on the gravestone erected by their son John on the Rock of Cashel. The father lived to the ripe age of seventy-four and Kate to eighty-six. John II also had erected a twin stone commemorating brother William, six years his senior, who died at age thirty-seven. The antique script carves a fraternal prayer in stone, "May the Lord have Mercy on his Soul. Amen."

The second John Walsh rented a large farm in the town of Ardmayle where he had been raised. He was a dairy farmer who, at one time, owned thirty-seven cows, a sign of prosperity. But even the most solid income would have been hopelessly stretched to support the seven sons and seven daughters born to him and his wife, Ann Maher.

Patrick's own father, also named Patrick, was the eleventh child in this family, arriving in 1849, when his father John was building a new house to be named "Suir View," after the river of that name that watered the valley. The baby's arrival caught the family between homes and this Patrick was born in temporary quarters in a converted factory on the bank of the river. Originally constructed as a woolen mill, the building had served as a temporary military barracks prior to the Walsh family moving in. Just behind it were the ruins of a Tudor-style manor built circa 1550 by a John Butler who had held the hereditary title, "Baron of Ardmayle." His descendant, Theobold, was hanged from the arch of the entrance gate in 1690 by the artillery men of the English King William. The elder Patrick played among these ruins where a child's cry provoked melodious echoes within the broken walls.

Recording much later in America the events of his own early life, son Patrick remembered stories his father had told him about this enormous family in Ardmayle. Four sons and a daughter departed for Australia, the first about 1860, part of the great wave of emigration that followed the devastations of the potato famine. The senior Patrick was a young boy when his brothers and sisters set out. The emigrants apparently succeeded in finding a new life in Australia since, in later years, they sent their father John gifts of money.

The eldest son of these fourteen siblings was the third John

Walsh, born in 1834, who attained a measure of distinction in Ireland in his lifetime. He became a regional manager for Charles Bianconi, an entrepreneur forty some years his senior. Bianconi had arrived in Ireland from Tregolo, Italy, in 1802 as a young boy, sent by a father determined to save him from conscription in the army. His early years as itinerant salesman for a picture shop, must have soured Bianconi on the primitive means of transportation available to any Irishman who had to take to the roads for a living. In 1815 he proposed a modest improvement by initiating a new type of horse-drawn car to carry passengers from Clonmel to Cahir in Tipperary, a distance of some ten miles. That proved but the beginning, and a chain of such routes was destined to spread all over Ireland, causing a minor revolution in national transportation.

It was Charles Bianconi who owned the farm in Ardmayle where John Walsh II and his wife Ann were raising their large family. Bianconi noticed the alertness and good sense of their oldest boy and brought him into his business. In the years that followed, Patrick's Uncle John took charge of the company's transportation lines in northern Ireland. When Bianconi began to divest himself of his transportation business in 1866, John bought a fleet of carriages with two hundred and eighty horses. A measure of John's prominence was his election as mayor of Sligo, the principal city in northwest Ireland.

About the time John (III) assumed charge of the horse and carriage business in the north, his employer, Charles Bianconi, re-claimed his farm properties in Ardmayle, obliging his tenants, John's parents, to leave Suir View. John II and Ann Walsh, with four sons and daughters still at home, moved to a small farm in neighboring Nodstown. The father soon found himself in debt and, for several years, lived a rather secluded life. He avoided visiting Cashel for fear of facing unpaid bills at the local stores. Ann passed away in late 1866, adding considerably to his loneliness.

It seems strange that the prosperous John III in the north did not take some action to help his father re-settle on another property and avoid debt. Many years later he erected an imposing monument on his parents' graves on the Rock of Cashel in memory of "his beloved mother" and "his beloved father," the lettering attests. Why John III did not aid his father when financially needy is unresolved.

After an extended period of semi-seclusion on his Nodstown farm, John II summoned the courage to travel the six miles into Cashel. When the shopkeepers asked him why he did not trade there anymore, John thought they were being sarcastic and responded angrily. One of the tradesmen caught onto the situation: "John, you don't owe a single penny to any man in town. Your children settled all your bills from Australia." The news moved the man to tears. His son, the elder Patrick, remembered the relief and renewed pride that filled his father as he told the family in the evening what had taken place that day in town.

While Patrick I passed on to son Patrick the story of older brother John, entrepreneur and mayor of Sligo, another brother Michael, was the source of a more exotic tale. Michael was six feet four and a soldier of fortune. His addiction to travel began when, before he was twenty, he joined a contingent of Tipperary recruits who set off for Italy to fight for the rights of Pope Pius IX against the nationalist Garibaldi. Returning to Ireland in 1860 at the end of an abortive campaign, he received from his father a piece of farmland in neighboring County Waterford.

A month after handing Michael this generous gift, John II had occasion to go to Waterford and stopped to visit his son on his new farm. He was shocked to discover that Michael had sold the farm and disappeared. Investigating further, John learned, to his dismay, that Michael had opted for steady travel by joining the British army. John II pursued the matter of Michael's whereabouts, directing a written inquiry to the War Office in London. The reply conveyed the information that Michael Walsh was not in the United Kingdom but the War Office would try to locate him in the colonies. A year elapsed before official word arrived that Michael was stationed in India as a sergeant in the Imperial Army.

The inquiry set in motion by his family got Michael into trouble. In tracing him to India, army authorities learned that the sergeant had neglected contacting his family for a period in excess of a year, a military offense at that time. Michael was demoted.

The setback seemed to have been temporary, and soon afterward Michael married an officer's widow. He continued his career in the British army for some twenty years and then returned to Ireland upon retirement. This was in the early 1880's and the young Patrick, then about thirteen, remembered the aura of adventure surrounding this veteran uncle of foreign wars. Many men left Ireland but few returned to give an accounting, and this uncle had spent his career in far-off, exotic India. Besides, he was the envy of the county for the government pension he now drew.

Nevertheless, Michael was hardly ready to settle back into rural Tipperary for any length of time. Having renewed his contacts with the local farmers who needed markets for their produce, he developed a role as a middleman in an import-export business. Before long he moved back to India, and his nephew's impression was that his business prospered there. Contracts arrived in Tipperary for the shipping of a thousand hogs a month or a thousand crates of eggs. At one point, Michael even wrote his brother Patrick urging him to allow young Patrick and younger brother Jack to join him in India. Apparently no serious thought was ever given that proposal. When Uncle Michael died several years later his widow stayed on in India as a boarder in a convent. Michael's Irish relatives believed that the couple died childless and left a significant sum of money. Inquiries from London came to Patrick I concerning Michael's surviving kin, but no money was ever received.

Patrick I, the eleventh of John II's fourteen children, had moved with his parents to the small farm in Nodstown in 1866, following the financial reversal that forced his father to give up his dairy farm. Adjoining this new property was the prosperous home of Thomas and Mary Coman, and Patrick often noted the comings and goings of visitors there. He was probably a youth of seventeen when he approached and introduced himself to his neighbor's niece, Ellen Burke. Ellen lived with her parents, sister and two brothers in Templederry, some thirty-five miles north of Nodstown, where her father operated a bakery. Although Ellen was nine years older than Patrick, the boy was husky and broad-shouldered and the two became friends.

Ellen's visits to her aunt increased as she and Patrick grew closer. Finally a marriage took place in the little country church of Boherlahan. The Reverend Maurice Duggan, Ellen's maternal uncle, could not make the trip from his parish in Liverpool, England, to perform the ceremony, but he did what meant more to the newly-weds. He sent them a sum of money that allowed them to buy a house and modest farm a few miles away in Ballydine. Its owner planned to emigrate to Australia and, in his urge to move on, sold the property below market value.

The home that Patrick and Ellen settled into was considerably larger than the one- or two-room cottages dotting the countryside. It was a sturdy structure with stone walls and a peaked slate roof that had originally been built as a police barracks. The front door opened into a rectangular room which they soon set up as a combination general store and pub. A door in the rear wall of this room opened in turn to a large kitchen which became the family living area. The upstairs had three bedrooms.

This hamlet of Ballydine numbered all of three homes. Its geographical position seemed secure, however, because the town of Cashel lay five miles away and its famous Rock was visible from the rise in the ground where the Walsh house stood. County Tipperary was in relative peace in 1868. The poverty that afflicted small farmers through most of Ireland was abated for those who owned land in the "Golden Vale" of Tipperary. The fertile soil of these southern valleys contrasted sharply with the rocky lands along the western coast.

In the autobiographical sketch of his early years, Patrick II wrote a description of the economic hardships of the Ireland of his birth:

> The nineteen years of my life spent in the fertile valley of the Golden Vale of Tipperary was at a time in history when 750 landlords owned fully one half of all Ireland and when 600,000 were tenant farmers struggling to eke out a bare existence on small rented parcels of ground seldom over 15 acres in area.

Holding the land at the will of the landlord, totally without capital, in constant arrears of rent, and with just a miserable, diseased potato patch between his family and starvation, the average farmer of this period presented, at best, a pitiful picture. The lime, or sometimes sod-walled and thatch-roofed one-storey building in which he lived was a sad commentary on the connotations usually associated with the word "home." Its small windows, with patched glass panes, admitted such little light that the paucity of house furnishings and the general bareness of the interior with its earthen floor were not too noticeable. Ample shadows, with a generosity and kindliness never to be equalled by the grasping landlord, quietly covered the harshness of penury so that even poverty could assume the semblance of dignity.

Although poverty was almost the rule of the day at this time, fortune had smiled gently on our family as it had on several others in this agrarian paradise of the Golden Vale. The relative financial success of the Walshes probably owed much to the superior fertility of this region.

The scene of Patrick's childhood was etched deeply in his memory because at the age of seventy-five he could describe it closely. The elevated vantage point of his Ballydine home

afforded a grand view in nearly every direction. To the southwest and about ten or eleven miles distant were the Galty Mountains, the second highest range in all Ireland. A little more distant and directly to the south, were the famed crags of the Knockmealdown Mountains that separate Tipperary from the County of Waterford. Closer at hand, about five miles southeast of our house was the ancient city of Cashel with its renowned "Rock" that has, through the ages, held a peculiar fascination. The Suir River lent its picturesque glistening splendor to the beauty of the scene as it wound its tortuous way through the valley.

Patrick was the oldest, born in September, 1868. Four siblings followed: John in 1870, Anna in 1872, Bridget, 1874, and Alice, 1877. Patrick I and Ellen managed the family enterprises in tandem. The husband worked the farm, planting mostly oats and barley. He also looked after a sizable herd of hogs and maintained the property.

Ellen tended the store and the pub. The younger Patrick later held that "there was a certain innate resourcefulness and business aptitude that urged the Walshes into any kind of activity where an honest profit could be realized." One example he gave was the contract held by his father and his grandfather before him for the repair of neighborhood roads. For a fifty-seven-year period, one and then the other engaged in this part-time work until finally another party underbid the family for the contract.

An additional business venture was collecting rents from tenant farmers in the area. Son Patrick was quick to point out in his memoirs that his father was in no way like "the frequently autocratic, self-interested, hard-hearted collector that too often oppressed his neighbors with a harshness that sometimes exceeded that of the absentee landlord." Rather, the elder Patrick was an outspoken defender of the tenant farmer, a stance that would later get him into trouble with the local authorities.

A general store and pub right in the house lent a busyness and sociability to the family life style. When the store closed for the day on its last customers, an evening clientele held forth in the bar. The front entrance into the large, rectangular room provided a natural division between the general store on the left and the tavern on the right. Raising five children while running a store and bar was work for more than one person, and Ellen had two neighborhood girls who regularly helped her with the chores.

The senior Patrick spent evenings chatting with the bar's patrons and enjoyed a local reputation as a colorful story teller. His son later recalled that sitting at the dinner table or in the bar with a few neighbors, his father, in his pleasant, quiet way of speaking

> seemed to take particular pleasure in repeating, and perhaps improvising, many of the ancient legends from which nearly all of Ireland has drawn a rich, if almost fantastic tradition. He would sit for hours or as long, in fact, as one or two listeners would sit with him and, in his deep tones, related stories and myths that went all the way back to the days of St. Patrick. It is

to these narratives that I owe whatever knowledge I have of my
forebears and their ancestry.

Within sight of the Walsh house was the thousand acre bog of
Ballymoor. It had excellent turf or peat and, especially in summer-
time, groups came from Cashel and even Clonmel, twenty-one miles
away, to cut turf as fuel for stoves. After a day's work, the men
gathered at the Walsh bar to drink porter and banter among themselves, bringing the family a brisk, seasonal business.

Patrick senior had another way of raising money on the bogs.
When a large group was cutting peat, he hitched a horse to the
jaunting car and rumbled off to the bakery in Cashel. There he
loaded up several large sacks of bread and filled a half-dozen jugs
with water. Son Patrick or Jack often went along for company.
Arriving back at the bog, young Patrick remembered how pleased the
perspiring turf cutters were to pause in the heat of the day and dig
down in a pocket or leather pouch for a pence to buy a loaf of bread
and take a long draught from one of the jugs which burlap had
insulated from the sun on the wagon floor.

It was on clear, sunny days that most of the turf-cutting was
done. Often whole families of Irish farmers worked together—the
men cutting and throwing up the wet turf from the ditch and the
women and children forming and molding the soggy mass into blocks
and laying them out to dry and harden in the sun prior to stacking.

Patrick recalled a favorite quip of his father's which seldom
failed to get a laugh from the laborers. "This is mighty good turf you
have here," he'd say to the newcomer. Usually there'd be a brief
assent at which the father would add, "I think you'll be getting twice
as much heat as you thought out of this turf." When the one
addressed looked puzzled, Patrick would blandly continue, "It'll warm
you next winter in the stove and it sure is warming you plenty today."

If Patrick senior had the business acumen that his son attributed
to the Walshes, it was pleasantly couched in an easy-going disposi-
tion. He seemed as attached to his porter and his stories as he was to
his business interests. When he went to collect a rent or retrieve a

borrowed farm tool, he seldom refused an invitation to sit down to tea. He had a peaceful way about him and was slow to identify any situation as an emergency.

Along with his mildness, however, Patrick was known beyond the family circle for his physical strength. His son remembered a vivid illustration. It was late in the fall of the year and Ellen had been after her husband for several weeks to ask their neighbor, Michael Ryan, to help slaughter a pig to hang for the winter. She needed lard and wanted to get busy with the lengthy process of rendering the fat on the kitchen stove.

Finally, somewhat annoyed by her insistence, Patrick went into the yard and butchered the creature alone. From years of experience he had attained such deftness in the use of the knife that the pig had not only been killed but was practically dressed before anyone in the household knew what was happening. When Ellen, young Patrick and Jack came to the back door, the father was already adjusting the wooden struts that would hold the hind legs apart when the pig was hoisted on the makeshift rack. His son recalled years later,

> I could see that my mother was pleased and she said to Dad in her sweet Irish voice, "Ye have done a fine job, Paddy, but how can we hang that fat creature without help? Sure he must weigh 250 pounds if he weighs an ounce." To this my father replied, "Don't worry your head about such things. I'll hang it myself, without Mike Ryan to help me."
>
> Having by this time finished the task of adjusting and tying the struts, my father bent down and raised the prostrate form with as little apparent effort as when he would lift my baby sister in his arms to kiss her. Shifting the animal above his head as a weight-lifter would do with a heavy bar, he was able to engage the leg struts and position the carcass on the wooden trellis. This being done, he turned and smiled blandly at all of us. Mother lit up and ran to him, "Sure it's a fortunate woman I am to have such a grand, strong husband." We all marvelled at his strength. It was the ease and nonchalance of it all that made him masterful in my eyes.

Yet it was only on occasion that the senior Patrick demonstrated this physical prowess. His normally gentle manner seemed to hinder his displaying it. His son remembered one context that got Patrick sufficiently agitated to suggest a potential for physical violence. This was when discussions turned to the subject of the tenant farmer and his plight. Although in 1870 and again in 1881 the British Parliament had passed Land Acts granting minimal protection from arbitrary eviction to the small tenant, there were ways for landlords to circumvent their obligations. Patrick's belief that the land was God's gift to mankind as a whole and not the domain of a privileged few made him an outspoken supporter of Parnell and the Land League.*

In the late 1880's, poor harvests drove agricultural profits down, resulting in an increase in evictions of tenants. A bitter struggle followed during which the elder Patrick spoke publicly against the evictions. In 1890, two years after the son had left for America, Patrick senior was arrested for inflammatory statements and sentenced to a year and half in prison.

In the younger Patrick's recollections of his boyhood in Ballydine, the image of a particular tree was important. A hundred and fifty feet from his house was a towering ash whose gnarled limbs reached some seventy feet into the air, almost grasping at the fleeting clouds above it. This giant tree was the last of five that had been planted two hundred years earlier at different locations in the area, each about a mile apart. This one was known locally as "the Walsh tree" and the four-year-old Patrick claimed it as his own, climbing and jumping in its lower branches. He was joined in his games by

---

* *Charles Stewart Parnell, the hero of Irish nationalism, was a principal figure in the Land League, founded in 1879 by Michael Davitt. Its aim was to improve the dire conditon of the Irish tenant farmer in three principal ways: 1) bringing about reductions in rent; 2) protecting those threatened with eviction; and 3) changing the law to allow a tenant to buy his land over time. The latter enshrined the principle of "land purchase" by which, during the next fifty years, a complete transfer of land ownership to the Irish peasantry took place. However, the Land League was itself suppressed by the British two years after it was founded.*

Timothy Murphy, his first real companion, whose family home was next door to the Walshes. The two competed in throwing stones high up into the branches in the futile hope that one would succeed in clearing it.

When they tired of challenging the tree, there were other activities to excite growing youngsters. The boys were enamored of the horses that carried customers to the Walsh store. They liked to pet them and question their owners about them. The pub itself supplied playing hoops from the half barrels of porter that abounded in any Irish public house of 1875. The hoops could be propelled by striking them with a stick and then running at their side to prevent their turning off course. The game was to see who could roll his hoop fastest and farthest. The course was generally from the ash tree downhill for a hundred yards to the blacksmith's shop that belonged to Michael Ryan, the third and last household of Ballydine. And if, by chance, Ryan was shoeing a horse, Patrick and Tim would linger there to watch.

Patrick was nine or ten when the Murphy family emigrated to America and Patrick had to part with his good friend. But Timmy was well gone before Patrick perceived any sadness in the event. In the weeks before the journey, fed by tales of the wonders of Boston that Timmy had heard from his father, both youngsters were caught up in the tremendous excitement of a boat trip across the Atlantic. Neither boy, however, was allowed to stay up for the "wake," the farewell party given by the neighbors on the eve of a departure for foreign shores. But the festivities took place in the Walshes' store-pub and Patrick lay awake upstairs keeping time in his head to the strains of music and the thud of dancing feet.

The events of the following day were clear in Patrick's mind six decades later. Spring was well advanced and the morning exceptionally bright. The elder Patrick was to drive the Murphy family and all their baggage to the train station of the Great Southern and Western Railroad at Gooldscross, two miles north. From there the family would have a seventy-five-mile train trip to Cobh, the port of Cork Harbor on Ireland's southern coast, which funneled the nineteenth century emigrant out of his country into the Atlantic and westward. To his delight, Patrick was allowed to squeeze into the overloaded jaunting car. The Murphys — mother, father and four youngsters — straddled the various shapes and forms of their luggage. Two huge trunks took up most room, each sealed with a shiny, tongue-shaped lock and dotted with polished metal rivets.

Patrick recalled years later how beautiful the countryside looked to him as the party jogged along behind Joe, the family roan. The distant mountains seemed purple and the green grasses of the fields were tall and lavish in their early growth. The carriage moved past large estates given over mostly to pasture where fine racing and hunting horses grazed. They also passed thatched cottages, potato patches and a few tumbledown churches. The excited chatter of the trip came to a halt at the first sight of the railroad station.

The bustling activity at Gooldscross distracted Patrick from any sad thoughts. Families gathered in tight little groups, bidding tearful good-byes to the son or neighbor setting out. The youngster thrilled at the sound of the oncoming train puffing into the station, its giant stack panting smoke. The Great Southern and Western Railroad, with its chugging locomotives, was among the most awe-inspiring things the world had yet shown him. Timmy was privileged to ride in such a magnificent machine and Patrick enthusiastically waved good-bye. But there had been tears in Mrs. Murphy's eyes as she embraced the two Patricks for the last time.

Father and son stood there until the last sight and sound had disappeared and then the elder Patrick had a few chores to perform before the ride home. It was during this pause that the youngster's enlivened imagination and high spirits began to settle. On the return trip he felt none of his earlier buoyancy. The empty jaunting car and the absence of his friend made him realize that his world had changed in the space of a brief hour. Even the countryside seemed less warm and colorful. The sky had clouded over and the distant Galty Mountains had changed their friendly purple to an indifferent gray. Finally, he mustered his composure and asked his father, "Isn't Dad Murphy ever going to come back again?" The negative answer was the seal, as it were, to the first deep emotional experience that Patrick could recall. Its forcefulness stayed with him with great clarity.

A year or two after the Murphys had departed, the other stalwart friend of Patrick's childhood, the giant ash tree, disappeared from his life as well. A dramatic story led to its removal. Some crime had been committed not far from Ballydine, though the boy was never certain of its exact nature. It was 1880, when the Land League was advocating a boycotting tactic against the land agents evicting tenant farmers. In fact, the tactic itself received its very name that year in Ireland. The first land agent in County Mayo who was isolated by his neighbors and denied all social and commercial contact was a man named Captain Boycott. The offense committed near Ballydine may have been related in some way to the wave of "boycotts" then occurring in the Irish countryside.

More important than the crime in this case was the punishment which far exceeded the wrongdoing and provoked angry reactions from the local population. One evening, a boisterous procession formed and a straw effigy of the judge was dragged to the ancient tree and hoisted high. Wood and turf were piled at the foot of the tree and ignited. The judge's effigy vanished in an instant but the flames continued to leap up and scorch the entire bark of the massive tree. Later on, the giant ash was felled and its charred remains carted away.

Even in those early years, when Patrick still had both Timmy Murphy and the ash tree, another element began to expand his world beyond the confines of Ballydine. The father started his two boys in school on the same day. Patrick was six and Jack scarcely four and a half. The school was two miles from home and situated in a modest structure of limestone walls and slated roof, a single room with three large windows front and back, and a fireplace and chimney at each end. Classes were held from ten in the morning until three in the afternoon, with the last half-hour devoted to religion. The few Protestant children in the group left at two-thirty.

The "Master," as teachers are known in Ireland, became an influence in Patrick's life. D.C. Maher, at nineteen perhaps the youngest graduate of the University College of Dublin, started teaching at the school two years before Patrick left it. Mr. Maher distinguished himself from most of the other schoolmasters. He was mild-mannered and understanding, administering discipline more with the positive force of his personality than with the arbitrary use of the rod. There were still courses left to pursue when Patrick reluctantly withdrew at the age of thirteen to start working full time on the farm. The Master had even helped him learn about new farming techniques, having introduced a course in agriculture, a very modern innovation in the curriculum of a rural Irish school of the 1880's.

The friendship between teacher and pupil survived their separation and the two corresponded even after Patrick's departure for America. On his first return to Ireland in 1927, at the age of fifty-eight, Patrick sought out his old Master and was welcomed by him as a returning son.

While growing up in Ballydine, Patrick and brother Jack liked to spend hours of their free time hunting and trapping in the local countryside. Along with their homemade traps and snares they took the family dog. Lacking a gun for shooting rabbits, the boys developed their own techniques. The dog was given the lead to first scare up an animal and chase it into a burrow. Plugging all possible exits except two, they flushed water into one end, driving the rabbit out of the other and into a sack. Patrick and Jack might wander some eight miles from home in pursuit of their quarry.

On occasions, the two would set out after dark, one carrying under his coat a huge turnip with its center scooped out to shelter a lit candle. This strange little entourage trudged along, protecting their light while looking for the resting places of blackbirds, plovers and other game birds. These made delicious eating when prepared by Ellen. Patrick and Jack also went in search of song birds. When captured alive, they could be sold, some to be shipped as far as Dublin where these little creatures were prized household pets. The handsome chaffinch was the most popular but goldfinches and bullfinches were also able songsters. The more common larks and thrushes had some value as well and in pursuing one of these, Patrick had a jarring experience.

With Jack's help he had constructed a trap out of twigs called a "crib" which had a trick door that automatically dropped when the hungry bird entered to retrieve the bait, usually a snail. One day Patrick returned to the site of one of his cribs and found a little woodthrush fluttering around inside. He lifted the gate and reached for the bird. The thrush hopped about to elude the groping hand and Patrick had to wrestle it still. In the tussle, the bird's neck was broken. Patrick remembered leaning against the tree for some time with the dainty bird in his hand, moving his finger gently over the soft feathers.

In fact, though he found hunting and trapping to be challenging and enjoyable, he always recalled that spontaneous twinge of remorse that gripped him at the sight of the inert form of any animal he had killed. He regretted snuffing out the intangible spark of life in some creature that had done him no harm. At one point he decided to talk to the parish priest about it. Father Hogan expounded the traditional theme of how the vegetable order is lower than the animal order and the animal order lower than man and that man, while respecting and not abusing the lower orders, had every right to use them for his sustenance. The conversation relieved Patrick's conscience somewhat but he admitted that it could not subdue the instinctive twinge he felt at the sight of any creature he had killed.

About the time Patrick left school to turn his attention to farming he became a warm enthusiast of Irish football.[2] The Ballydine Rovers of 1884-1890 became one of the more famous teams of the time and prominent in the Gaelic Athletic Association. Patrick loved football and claimed he would rather play than eat or sleep. He achieved a lowly berth on the team at age thirteen and gradually earned a place in the regular lineup. Though not tall, the boy was quick and could dart and shift around his opponents. This ability made him useful offensively and earned him a reputation for being a good point-getter.

It was after a particularly vicious match between teams from Tipperary and Waterford in 1884 that the soon-to-be-famous Gaelic

Athletic Association was formed. Although the new group aimed at standardizing football rules and reducing the violence endemic to the game as the Irish played it, the Gaelic Athletic Association had other goals as well. It meant to remedy "a parlous state of national pastimes and the consequent decline in national virility and to replace tennis, croquet, cricket, polo and other foreign and fantastic field sports by Gaelic football and hurling." Founded under the patronage of Archbishop Croke of Cashel, its membership grew to a peak of 52,000 by 1889, "spreading a simple pride in Irish consciousness for its own sake over large areas of the countryside."[3]

The Ballydine Rovers took part in many championships and tournaments sponsored by the Association, several in Ballydine itself. These tournaments were not simply football games, but more like carnivals, with exhibits and shows and a general community "day out." Local lore has it that 10,000 people attended one of these Ballydine hooplas. The Walsh pub must have made record sales that day.

Although Patrick liked nothing better than to play football, he could be an avid spectator if given the chance to attend a good match. At seventeen he walked eleven miles to see action by first-string teams of the Gaelic Athletic Association. The players were from Dublin and Patrick claimed he would have hiked to that game had the distance been twice as far.

Most of the stories Patrick remembered of his boyhood friendships centered around Tim Murphy. At the same time, Michael and Catherine Ryan were raising a family of ten children—five girls alternated with five boys—just two doors away. Patrick had first been attracted to the Ryans because of the noisy activity of the blacksmith's shop. Of all Mike Ryan's children, however, Patrick gradually developed his closest friendship with Mary Ann who was five years his senior. She was tall for her age, or at least the younger boy always fancied her that way. Her eyes and hair were dark and she moved with a certain natural grace. Patrick began to worship her and sought her out when he wanted help with school work. But by the time he was fifteen, a husky farmer and football player, there was a discernible change in their relationship. Years later he wrote, "She was the lady of my heart from as far back as I can remember – she never had a rival."

Even before he left school, Patrick had developed a strong interest in farming. It was not only the fact that the family owned land which he, as the eldest son, was expected to work. He loved the soil and the planting and harvesting of crops and even found satisfaction in the physical effort that farming demanded. A rich topsoil running from ten inches to a foot deep in the "Golden Vale" of Tipperary was a stimulus to any farmer's efforts.

Spring came early in the moderate Irish climate and plowing could be finished by mid-March. This was especially true if one had equipment to work with. Patrick senior had bought a new ten-inch plow and the son took particular delight in seeing how much ground he could cover with it in a single day. This drive to accomplish, however, did not seem to block his awareness of what was happening around him. With the poetic eye for detail that he never lost, he described his experience:

> Walking behind the horse, I loved to watch the sod roll over in an endless, snake-like curl, sliding off the moldboard in an intriguing twisting motion and lying in meticulous rows in the trail behind me. I sometimes looked to the rear to note the sparrows and robins which hopped into the furrow the plow had left to gobble up or carry off some tasty worm or grub. The occasional jolt of striking a stone or the hard tug through some heavily rooted growth meant that, by nightfall, my arms would be aching and my body tired; but for me this was a satisfying exhaustion, one that represented real work done.

Owning a plow and wanting to keep it busy, Patrick hired himself out to work neighboring farms as well. His plowing started at daybreak and continued as long as daylight permitted, until the sun dipped behind the peaks of the Galty Mountains. At noontime he took a break, coming home for lunch when he was working closeby or carrying a sandwich when his job was a few miles away. Sometimes one of his sisters brought lunch to him in the fields. On rarer occasions, Mary Ann Ryan carried it to him and would stay and chat as he ate. He remembered how he would chew his food slowly to delay her departure as long as possible.

After plowing came the harrowing to break up the clods and, finally, the seeding. For the most part, a grass seed was used or a grain such as oats or barley. Lacking a horse-drawn seed drill, the boy slung a bag around his shoulder. With daily practice he developed the slow, swinging gait synchronized with the rhythmic movement of the arm and hand to broadcast seeds in an even arc at each step forward. The same seed bag which felt so light in the morning freshness weighed like a stone by evening. On one day he was able to sow eight acres and earned himself a half crown. The plaudits of his parents and his brother Jack made him feel even richer.

As summer progressed, so did the amount of work, with hay to be mowed and grain reaped. Sometimes when weather conditions were just right, there would be second plantings in July. One year, spring came so early, followed by the perfect amounts of rain and sunshine, that three successive crops of hay were taken in before the return of cold weather.

As Patrick became a seasoned farmer, he gained proficiency in operating the reaper/thrasher. He enjoyed this work more than the plowing and seeding because he saw the harvest as the final goal achieved, the culmination of all his efforts.

He was just past his nineteenth birthday when an incident occurred that, without prior warning, irreversibly altered the course of Patrick's future. The Green family from the other side of Cashel had acquired a three horse-drawn reaper. The boy was irked by this and could no longer take the same pride in his own smaller apparatus. Besides, he could rationalize that with superior equipment a lot of extra work would get done. Learning that the Greens wanted to sell their prized reaper, Patrick hurried to convince his father that the family could really profit by buying it. The elder Patrick agreed to talk to the Greens the very next day.

In the morning Patrick headed for the fields in high spirits. All day he measured in his mind's eye the extra work he would accomplish with the new piece of equipment. He decided to quit the job a full hour early in the hope of trying out the new reaper before dark. At very least he could look it over.

Arriving home he passed the barn and saw his dad's horse tethered and fed but no sign of the new purchase. Then he remembered — why hadn't he thought of it before — how could one horse have pulled that large a piece of equipment? Probably he and his father would take the other horses and pick it up the first thing in the morning.

Patrick entered the house by the rear kitchen door. As he kissed his mother he detected a little tension in the soft lines of her face. He washed his hands and, as he dried them, inquired about the reaper. Ellen shook her head. "What happened?" he asked. "Wouldn't they sell it?" His mother kept cutting the vegetables in front of her. "Oh, they wanted to sell it all right. In fact, it was sold before your father got there."

The boy felt the blood rush to his head. "Didn't Dad get there early?" She still didn't look up and her voice was uncertain. "Well, he thought he'd stop at Sullivans' to collect the rent since it was on his way. They got talking a bit and he stayed for lunch."

Patrick could hardly believe what he heard. How could his father be so lethargic about a matter so important to his family's interests? It was an unpardonable sin. When the elder Patrick appeared in the kitchen, the boy made no effort to conceal his anger. The father apologized, but his unruffled attitude only increased the son's rage. In a split second young Patrick made a decision. "I'm going to America," he fairly shouted. "There I'll be able to buy all my own equipment."

They ate the evening meal in constrained silence. Sister Anna tried to break the tension by casual conversation but to no avail.

After supper, the father signaled Patrick to come outside and take a walk with him. Daylight was fading as they moved along the dirt road. The elder Patrick talked seriously and with an intensity that seldom surfaced. He was really sorry about the reaper and he would try his best to locate another one.

But young Patrick was adamant. It might have been his Irish obstinacy; it might have been that secretly, almost unconsciously, he had been longing for the adventure that a new land promised and to which so many he knew had already set out. He returned to the house unmoved in his decision. The tears and pleadings of his mother depressed him but did not alter his determination. He had made up his mind and there was no turning away. He would write frequently; he might even return before long. But he was resolved that he would depart for America, and as soon as possible.

The stubborn independence Patrick showed his parents had most likely been growing in step with the new insights he was gaining into his own abilities. On the farm in Ballydine he had been proving to himself and to the rest of his circumscribed world that he could be the most productive farmer around and he would do even more with better equipment. But his father had thwarted him and perhaps the incident was intensified by the son's memory of past occasions when he had resented his father's easy ways and lack of personal drive. Patrick already had thoughts of going to America, the appeal becoming stronger with each new departure of a friend or acquaintance. The conflict with his father was now a catalyst for decision. He had no idea how he would earn a living in America, but he felt that he would discover this on his own, without a father to assist him, without a father to impede him.

CHAPTER TWO

The Struggle for New York Roots

1888 - 1901

The journey to America for Patrick Walsh followed the same route his friend Tim Murphy had taken some ten years earlier. He caught the train at Gooldscross two miles from Ballydine, going the seventy-five miles to Cobh, port city of County Cork on Ireland's southwestern coast. Given the circumstances of his departure, he refused to take money from his father and had with him only the five pounds he had collected from a neighbor for cutting hay. After boarding the ship, Patrick pressed with other passengers against the rail for a last view of Ireland, the hills of Cobh dotted with homes and churches.

After what he later described as "an immoderately rough voyage in an antique tub," Patrick's ship docked at the tip of Manhattan about March 20, 1888, and discharged its weary passengers into the chill interior of Castle Garden. Originally built in 1811 as Castle Clinton, a fort for protection against incursions of the British navy, the structure was roofed over in the 1840's and converted into a theater named Castle Garden, with seating for 6,000. Although wrestling, bare-fisted boxing and even dog fights had been staged there, for a while it served as an opera house where the celebrated Jenny Lind gave a concert in 1850. By 1855, however, its doors were sealed to the public and the thick-walled circular stone bastion became the immigrant landing depot for New York City, precursor of Ellis Island. The open tract surrounding it soon was a haven for "runners" who were known to approach bewildered Irish and German newcomers, directing them for a fee to nonexistent lodgings.

Once he was processed by the New York Immigration Author-

ity, showered and disinfected, Patrick had to face the key problem
that had worried him throughout the voyage: how could he devise a
way to gain entry? Immigrants who arrived without a substantial
amount of money or a written contract for employment were not
permitted to leave the depot until called for by friends or relatives
who could vouch for their support. Patrick had none of these things
and the only account of what followed is his own.

"Hour after hour I sat," he recalled years later, "and never a
word was spoken for me. Finally, from the end of the hall, a lady's
sweet voice called out, 'Patrick, Patrick, are you there?' 'Mither of
mine, I come,' I replied, and I arose and departed. I was gone before
they knew what happened."[1]

Patrick's story, told some fifty years after his arrival at Castle
Garden, had probably been dramatized or embellished for his listeners' ears. But the probability exists that a stroke of luck solved his
problem and that an unknown person, in search of her own relative,
became his unwitting accomplice for slipping by the authorities.

Freed from the immigrant's "no man's land," Patrick hastily
crossed what is now Battery Park and stepped onto the streets of
Lower Manhattan. The scene that greeted him exceeded all prior
imagining. Buildings five and six stories tall, horse carriages jamming
the streets, pushcarts and vendors and the crush of pedestrians stopped
the young immigrant short. In his nineteen years he had never
visited even the larger Irish cities of Dublin and Cork. New York was
already close to one and a half million and one of the world's largest
commercial centers.

Patrick arrived on the eve of the city's physical transformation.
It is believed that no other metropolis underwent such visible change
in so short a time as did New York in the last decade of the century.[2]
Trinity Church steeple still dominated the skyline that greeted Patrick
in March of 1888. Just three months later, however, a ground-
breaking ceremony would be held for the Tower Building, which
rose to eleven stories upon completion in 1889 at 50 Broadway. And,
in 1890, the reign of the Trinity Church steeple over the New York
skyline would end forever as the 309-foot Pulitzer Building stretched

an unprecedented twenty-six stories above street level.

Recalling his arrival in later years, however, it was the weather rather than the size and bustle of the city that had made the more lasting impression. What remained of the famed blizzard of 1888 lay in mounds of snow along the curbs. Beginning March 11, snow had fallen for thirty hours, blanketing New York with an estimated four feet. Seventy-mile-per-hour winds had stacked drifts to the second story of buildings. "I was sorry I missed it," he reminisced. "Every soul in New York talked of it for weeks."

It is only conjecture where Patrick may have headed in search of a room for the night. He knew he had to conserve his limited cash until he could find a job. Not all city dwellers were well off — he could read that much in the dress and appearance of many who brushed by him as he manœuvered his way uptown. Quite possibly Patrick had some relative to look up on that first night, some contact among the many countrymen who preceded him.

Job hunting during those first weeks in the "land of opportunity" was frustrating and disappointing. Wherever he found a "Help Wanted" sign, there were many other applicants ahead of him. After a week of searching in vain he learned that farm hands were being hired on Staten Island and decided to pursue the occupation he knew best. It was hardly what he had in mind for the start of his career in New York City, but his funds were running out and he was beginning to feel desperate.

John Darcey's dairy farm was spread over property that forty-five years later would become the site of the Willowbrook State Hospital for the mentally retarded. Hay and grain were raised for feed so that, between the milking of the cows and the field work, Patrick resumed the farmer's long hours and hard labors. He persevered from May through September of 1888, from planting to harvest time. By then he had enough. Frustrated at being so close to Manhattan, yet isolated in a rural environment, he swore to himself as he left Staten Island, in a phrase his children would jokingly repeat, "May my right hand wither before I grab another cow by the udder."

As much as Patrick had appreciated the rewards of farming in

Ireland, he never contemplated doing the same in the new country. The years of homesteading and free government land grants in America were well over and possibly he thought a simple farmhand without capital had no future and could never earn enough to buy land for himself. Now, in September, 1888, he returned to New York City to look for a job, any job, just to gain a footing.

Patrick's first days back in Manhattan proved to him once again the difficulty of putting down his roots there. Job seekers outnumbered every opening and he felt the lack of friends or connections who might lend a helping hand. Finally he registered at an employment agency and was advised of a gardener-caretaker position on the estate of a family named Gillespie near Morristown, New Jersey. This offer would remove him even farther from city lights than Staten Island had, but his cash was nearly gone and he decided to take the job. Packing the same few belongings he had carried with him from Ireland, he ferried to Hoboken and boarded the train for Morristown.

In the hour's ride, Patrick struggled to sort out his confused feelings. He had broken relations with his beloved family in Ireland and had left behind the woman whom he wanted to marry. Contrary to his dream of getting settled quickly and proving how well he could make a new life on his own, he was now heading away from New York City and toward a job that held no promise of advancement in income or status. He felt himself a victim of circumstance and wondered how he could begin to control his own life. But of one thing he was certain. He was not yet ready to give up and return to Ireland.

Despite his misgivings, Patrick stayed working on the Gillespie estate for three years. Tending the grounds meant heavy work with little free time and he remarked later that the fifty cents a day hardly kept him in shoe leather. The reason he remained as long as he did was, in all likelihood, the friendships he formed there. The estate employed a number of gardeners and farmhands and Patrick took a particular liking to Mr. Lowry, the foreman, who lived with his family on the grounds. In later years, Patrick made several visits from Brooklyn to Morristown with his own family to visit the Lowrys who continued living on the estate for many years.

Four decades later, Patrick, as Commissioner, made an appearance at a Volunteer Firemen's Convention in Somerville, New Jersey. On the return trip, his chauffeur took a route that passed near Morristown. Patrick noticed some familiar landmarks and directed his driver to the road that led past the old Gillespie estate. To his astonishment, the sign above the entrance read "Villa Walsh." He later learned that the property had been purchased by a Bishop Walsh of Trenton and given to an Italian order of Sisters who named the house after their benefactor. Patrick was delighted at the unwitting memorial.

Patrick quit his job in Morristown just before Christmas of 1891 and moved back to New York. There was reason. Mary Ann Ryan had agreed to come to America to marry him. The two had corresponded since Patrick had left home three and a half years earlier. Life on the estate had been lonely for a young man, despite the friendships he had formed. Patrick urged Mary Ann to emigrate and take her chances with him.

Michael and Catherine Ryan were opposed to their eldest daughter's departing alone for a distant country. There would be little chance of ever seeing her again. One could mourn the departure of a son but, at the same time, understand its inevitability. His livelihood depended on it. The case of a daughter was different. What kind of life could she expect to find with Patrick Walsh, five years her junior, who had not advanced himself after three years in America? Had he stayed in Ireland at least he would have inherited a fairly prosperous farm. But Mary Ann Ryan was now twenty-eight years old and she had made up her mind. Her grief at crossing the will of her parents did not deter her from setting out.

Though they may not have viewed it as such, Mary Ann's separation from home was an act of rebellion, just as Patrick's had been earlier. And the Ryans and Walshes had other rebellious children. In 1892, the same year Patrick and Mary Ann were married in Brooklyn, Timothy, Mary Ann's handsome, twenty-one year-old brother, eloped with Bridget, Patrick's eighteen year old sister. When they ran off to Queenstown, both fathers pursued them to be sure they got married and to offer them land and home if they would stay in Ireland. Instead the couple sailed for America. Tim surprised his cousin Edward Maher by arriving on his Brooklyn doorstep with a young bride. It was Edward who would soon marry Patrick's other sister, Anna, who had already come to the States, probably living at the time with some of the large Maher family on Henry Street in Brooklyn. Anna, twenty, had mixed reactions to her younger sister's surprise arrival. Bridget's coming meant only fifteen year-old Alice remained to help her mother on the Ballydine farm.

In 1952, sixty years after this episode, a grandaughter of Timothy and Bridget, on a visit to Ireland, was introduced to Tim's sister, Johanna. The old lady smiled and sighed, "Yes, it was a terrible thing he did to run off with Bridget Walsh."

In a span of four years several young adults in the two families had taken a stand against their parents in order to pursue the romance or adventure or challenge that beckoned them. Ironically, in the years that followed, Patrick and Mary Ann would imbue in their children the virtue of unquestioning obedience to authority. Their moral legacy to the next generation would certainly not include the spirit of rebellion. Whether purposefully or not, that tide was stemmed.

Patrick's immediate concern upon returning to New York City in late 1891 was to find the employment that had eluded him twice before. This time he was more fortunate; the Union Ferry Company took him on as a deck hand.

The inauguration of a steam-operated ferry line between Brooklyn and New York in 1814, making daily commutation possible between the then two cities, launched Brooklyn Heights as New York's first suburb. The Union Ferry Company, in 1891, operated five separate ferry lines linking Brooklyn with Lower Manhattan. Each line had its own slips and ferryhouses and was named after its destination on the New York side. The Fulton Ferry line, the earliest and best known, linked Fulton Street, Brooklyn, with Fulton Street, New York. Patrick worked north of this on the Catherine Street

Ferry, carrying passengers from a slip in the shadow of the Brooklyn Bridge tower on the Brooklyn side across the East River to the slip at the foot of Catherine Street and the shadow of the bridge tower on the New York side. A total of thirteen ferry boats plowed the East River on their five separate courses, bearing names like *Mineola, Montauk, Clinton* and *Winona.*

A visiting Englishman in 1869 gave this colorful account of the Brooklyn ferries and very likely Patrick witnessed the same scene when he went aboard in 1891.

> What are these huge castles rushing madly across the East River? Let us cross in the Montauk from Fulton Ferry and survey the freight. There are fourteen (horse) carriages and the passengers are countless — at least 600. Onward she darts at headlong speed until, apparently in perilous proximity to her wharf, a frightful collision appears inevitable. The impatient Yankees press — each to be the first to jump ashore. The loud "twong" of a bell is suddenly heard; the powerful engine is quickly reversed, and the way of the vessel is so instantaneously stopped that the dense mass of passengers insensibly leans forward from the sudden check.[3]

Once these passengers were ashore in Brooklyn, the loading gates at the ferryhouse swung open and another crowd heading for Manhattan pressed forward from the waiting room: clerks, shop girls, day laborers with lunch pails, storekeepers, barbers and business people.

In the decade before Patrick began work as a ferryhand, a separate and significant link between the cities had been established. The Brooklyn Bridge had emerged as the greatest engineering feat of its era and, during the eight years since its opening, had become the principal conduit for horse carriage traffic, train riders and pedestrians moving between Brooklyn and New York. By 1888, the trains over the bridge were carrying thirty million passengers a year.[4] Still, as the city of Brooklyn grew at an amazing rate, more than doubling its population between 1870 and 1890, one bridge could not sustain the volume of commuter traffic. The Williamsburg Bridge was added in 1903 while the ferry lines kept up a busy service until the first subway tunneled its way under the East River in 1908.*

As a newly-hired deck hand, Patrick crossed the river forty times a day, helping to dock and undock the lurching boat as it bounced from pile to pile. On these countless trips the Irishman developed his life-long attachment to the harbor of New York, the salt air, the ships of all sizes that plied the river and to the Brooklyn Bridge which cast its dramatic shadow over his ferry route. He had ample time to study the New York skyline and, as a way of passing the time, he learned to identify every building in sight. In later years, as the Manhattan skyline was transformed, he made a point of keeping an updated tally of all new buildings.

Patrick and Mary Ann were married in St. Charles Borromeo church on January 27, 1892. Belonging to a parish was always key to the Irish immigrant's sense of identity and the parish life of St. Charles would be important to the couple for their entire lives. They moved into rented rooms at 24 Hicks Street, some ten blocks north of the church, on the fringe of the Brooklyn Heights area and a stone's throw from the tower of the Brooklyn Bridge.** Patrick had an easy walk from his apartment to the ferry slip.

Things seemed to be finally coming together for the young immigrant after four years in America. He was no longer alone, having succeeded in marrying his childhood sweetheart. He had found a job in New York which finally ended his rural isolation. The city offered all kinds of human contact and more stimulation than he had ever known. Not least of the advantages was exposure to the Irish community which was predominant in many neighborhoods around the city. On one occasion Patrick traveled to Gaelic Park at

---

The last trip of the Fulton Ferry, the only remaining line, occurred in 1924.

**The house was torn down in the 1940's to make way for the Brooklyn-Queens Expressway.*

Broadway and 240th Street in The Bronx to watch an Irish-American football team take on local rivals. Patrick talked to the players who had heard of his Ballydine football team in Tipperary. On that particular Sunday, the Irishmen were short a man and the sturdy-looking Patrick was invited to fill in. He never forgot that he scored the only two points of the game.

But soon Patrick found that he had little time for his well-loved football. Two sons were born while the couple lived on Hicks Street — a namesake Patrick in late 1892 and Michael in early 1894. The quarters on Hicks Street became too small for their needs and by mid-year the family had rented a larger apartment at 70 Joralemon Street. This move brought them into the heart of the Brooklyn Heights neighborhood where they would remain for fifty-two years. The Irish immigrants had set down roots in Brooklyn.

In fact, the massive waves of Irish immigration to America in the nineteenth century had been a major influence in the radical transformation of Brooklyn from a small village to a major city. The same ferry lines that permitted residence in Brooklyn to bankers and stock brokers also transported the immigrant to unskilled jobs in commerce and industry. More than half of Brooklyn's resident wage earners, however, were employed in Brooklyn itself, with well under half commuting to New York.[5] By 1855, Brooklyn was the third largest city in America and a major manufacturing center. It contained eight miles of piers, dry docks, grain elevators and warehouses. "It was a larger seaport than New York, a larger city than Boston, Chicago, St. Louis, San Francisco, and growing faster than any of them."[6]

Although by 1890 the Germans had replaced the Irish as the largest group of new immigrants settling in Brooklyn, the Irish continued to be a major presence.[7] One area in particular, between Fulton Street and the Navy Yard where large numbers of people had been crammed into tenement buildings, was pejoratively labeled "Irishtown." But it was in Brooklyn Heights, and not Irishtown, that the young Walsh family settled. Perhaps it was the area's proximity to the ferryhouse where Patrick worked that first attracted him. Though a dozen blocks away, he would cover the distance in a fast, steady clip. He loved a long walk and, when his work moved to Lower Manhattan, his unbroken stride carried him over the Brooklyn Bridge and into the city. He still held this in common with the Tipperary farm boy who could hike six miles to plow a field or eleven to watch a football game.

In the area called Brooklyn Heights, some eight blocks wide and fourteen long, lived Brooklyn's oldest and wealthiest families. From 1820 until the Civil War, Brooklyn and Brooklyn Heights were synonymous in the popular mind. Certainly it was the unchallenged social, cultural and moral center of Brooklyn, the latter enhanced by the fame of Plymouth Church and its charismatic preacher Henry Ward Beecher. But Patrick and his family were not pioneers in penetrating this enclave of the locally established, monied class. By the 1890's, newly-arrived immigrants had already made inroads and many of the stately old brownstones had deteriorated into rooming houses or were subdivided into apartments. These tended to be concentrated in the south Heights, although there were other streets where old-guard inhabitants and newcomers almost rubbed elbows.

A third son, John, arrived in November of 1895. In contrast to his robust older brothers, John was sickly from birth and it was uncertain if he would survive the first months of infancy. His skin was extremely delicate and Mary Ann constantly rubbed it with oil. For fear of bone protrusion, he was carried about on a pillow until the skin texture gradually strengthened.

Patrick was advanced to ferry toll collector and now earned seventy-five dollars a month. Mary Ann was pregnant again and, in 1896, the family moved to 298 Henry Street, a three-story attached building between Atlantic Avenue and State Street. At 298 they occupied the third floor and there seven children would be born during the following ten years. The ground floor housed a saloon and three separate families lived on the three floors above. Since Patrick had grown up in Ireland with the family-run pub at the front of his house, he probably saw nothing objectionable in raising his family just two floors above a similar establishment.

Relatives were neighbors now. Patrick and Mary Ann most likely discovered this new apartment through Mary Ann's cousin, Kate Maher, married to Jerome Breen and living on the floor below. The adjacent brownstone at 296 was occupied by others of the large Maher family. Patrick's sister Anna married Edward Maher that year and moved to Flatbush. Timothy and Bridget Ryan, the young couple who had eloped to American four years earlier, were busy raising children on 18th Street in Manhattan, over the blacksmith shop Tim established like his father in Ballydine. Blacksmiths made a decent living in the city at the turn of the century since horses were crucial to the transportation of people and goods alike.

Shortly after the move to Henry Street, a happening at the Union Ferry Company changed the direction of Patrick's career. An opening developed for the position of ferry captain and Patrick, who had been working for the company for five years, went into the office to inquire about it. The manager he spoke with made no effort to gloss over the facts. Although Patrick had a good record as an employee, he would waste his time filing an application for captain unless he were willing to join the Order of Masons.* For Patrick this was a direct insult to his Catholic faith and he walked off the job the same day.

With three children at home and a fourth on the way, the young Irishman could not have afforded the luxury of quitting work, even in moral protest. Most likely he already had another prospect in mind. Mrs. Thomas Foley had been one of his ferry boat customers. In his friendly, gregarious way he had chatted with passengers, especially those who ferried back and forth with some regularity. Mrs. Foley had let him know that her husband was the Tammany boss of the Fourth Ward in lower Manhattan and that Patrick should call on him if ever in need of help. Now he was really in need.

Tom Foley, Tammany Hall's man-on-the-spot in lower Manhat-

---

* *Freemasonry, traditionally condemned by the Catholic church, was a worldwide secret society that adopted the rites and trappings of ancient religious orders. Masons were influential in many American businesses at the turn of the century and into the next several decades.*

tan, was a powerful figure in the Democratic party at the turn of the century.[8] To this day, Foley Square memorializes him. Although by the early 1920's Big Tom Foley would be reputed to be the principal protector of the underworld in Manhattan, history probably remembers him best as the individual responsible for introducing Al Smith into political life. Always a judge of talent, Foley spotted Smith when the latter was a young laborer in the Fulton Fish Market. With Foley's backing, Smith took his first steps in politics which eventually led him to serve four terms as New York State governor.

In 1896, the year Tom Foley assigned the twenty-two year-old Smith his first political "contract" or errand, the boss also hired Patrick Walsh as bartender in the saloon he then owned on South Street near the Manhattan side of the Brooklyn Bridge.* Patrick stayed with that job a full five years. He was familiar with the operation of a pub from the one his family owned in Ballydine but he was not as comfortable in this environment as his patient, talkative father had been. Nevertheless, he was dealing with a familiar Irish clientele, recent arrivals in lower Manhattan.

Patrick opened the bar in the morning and closed it again at night, often quite late. The bartender not only served drinks but prepared the free lunch offered bar customers at noontime — homemade soups, cheese and crackers. He learned to make a delicious chowder with clams fresh from the neighboring Fulton Street Fish Market.

At home a fourth son, Jeremiah, was born in January of 1897. But the parents' joy in their growing family was shattered later that year by the illness their oldest boy developed. Young Patrick had just passed his fifth birthday and was showing signs of being the most gifted of the children. He liked to pore over the daily newspaper, trying to recognize words and, with coaching from his parents, was

---

* *In 1941, Al Smith was a speaker at the testimonial dinner given Patrick on his 40th anniversary in the Fire Department. On that occasion, Smith reminisced about the early days when a unit of Tammany revolved around Tom Foley's pub.*

already building his vocabulary. Mary Ann often sent him down to the stores along Atlantic Avenue and he would come bounding back, excited to have managed the correct purchase and change.

No record is left of what childhood sickness took the youngster's life. The death in December of 1897 apparently followed only a few weeks of illness. As at other times of deep emotion later in life, Patrick found an outlet for his sorrow in writing verse.

> Why should I feel lonely
> When the moon is shining bright?
> Why should tears come to my eye
> When clouds obscure its light?
> I am thinking sadly of such another night,
> When clouds were moving lazily
> And the moon shone just as bright
> How I listened to the prattle
> Of a darling little boy
> Whose shouts of merry laughter
> So filled my heart with joy.
> How strange the questions that he asked
> 'Twas "how" and "when" and "why"
> They came to place the moon man
> So far up in the sky.

In the second stanza, the father assures himself that all his son's questions are finally answered, for the Lord, who had given the boy for just a while, had taken him back again.

Mary Ann had been pregnant when young Patrick died and, in May of 1898, gave birth to the couple's first daughter, Ellen. Their happiness at adding a girl to the family was still shadowed by their recent loss of their son. The following year yet another girl arrived — Catherine — in July of 1899.

During the spring of the year 1900 Patrick's younger brother Jack appeared unannounced at the front door. Jack was now in his late twenties and had developed a wanderlust reminiscent of his paternal Uncle Michael. Patrick and Mary Ann were elated at seeing him and hearing news of family and friends around Ballydine. There had been occasional letters back and forth, but neither the Walshes nor the Ryans had reconciled themselves to the departure of their children. Patrick had left in anger, critical of his father's attitudes and mode of living. The son could not in any way apologize for the position he had taken. The past was now behind him. Yet he carried with him a loyal affection for the family he had left, as Mary Ann did for hers. Their feelings were reflected in the naming of their first two sons and two daughters after their parents: Patrick and Michael for their fathers, Ellen and Catherine for their mothers.

Jack must have told the full story of their father's imprisonment some years before for his outspoken support of Parnell and the Land League. Ellen Walsh had managed to keep the family business going by herself for those eighteen months and Jack had taken care of the farm work. Now he stayed for a couple of weeks in New York, spending time with the families of his brother and his two sisters, and seeing the sights of the city. He departed as abruptly as he had arrived. To Patrick's shock a few days later, he received a telegram from the upstate city of Troy, advising him that his brother had died there without burial arrangements. Borrowing the money he thought he would need, Patrick got Tim Ryan to go with him on the 150 mile train trip.

Because of the time that had elapsed, the casket could not be opened, but the local authorities turned over Jack's wallet and identification found on the body. Patrick had a funeral mass said in Troy and buried his brother in a small plot he purchased locally. Once back in Brooklyn, he had another mass said for Jack at St. Charles and sent money to have additional masses offered in Ireland.

More startling news arrived two weeks later. Jack had turned up safely in Ireland. Doubtlessly, a pickpocket on the streets of New York had relieved him of his wallet before he boarded the ship. As a result, Patrick had unwittingly provided some thief or hobo with a Christian burial in Troy. After the relief of learning that Jack was alive and the chagrin at having spent money they could not afford, Patrick and Mary Ann could only laugh. It was a story they laughed at through every retelling.

Like his Uncle Michael before him, the wandering Jack eventually enlisted in the British army. He was well into his forties when killed in action at the Battle of Mons in Belgium during World War I and was buried in Le Havre. A medal of honor from the British government was mailed to the Walsh family homestead in Ballydine where Alice, the youngest, still lived. She forwarded to Patrick this sole memento of the inscrutable Jack.

While Patrick and Mary Ann were enjoying their expanding family circle, a series of misfortunes took place in their Henry Street apartment that tried their faith and hope and made them seriously think of giving up and returning to Ireland.

Bacillary dysentery is no longer a term that sparks panic in the hearts of parents. As the twentieth century advanced and sanitation standards improved, many previously common bacterial infections were eradicated. But, at the turn of the century, epidemics occurred frequently in overcrowded areas with inadequate sanitation. Young children were the susceptible victims, adults being more resistant to this type of infection. Its onset was sudden, with fever, irritability, vomiting, diarrhea and abdominal pain. Weight loss and dehydration became severe and an afflicted child was likely to die within twelve days.

The breeding ground for the bacteria on the third floor of 298 Henry Street was probably the milk that stood about in open cans after delivery. The weather had turned hot in June of 1900, not long after Jack's dramatic departure. When the eleven-month-old Catherine contracted dysentery, the parents hovered about the feverish baby, trying every remedy recommended by doctor and neighbors. But the child succumbed to the dogged course of her illness and died within two weeks.

Some welcomed comfort arrived that summer in the visit of Mary Ann's father. Probably it was the fact that two of his children now lived in New York that motivated Michael Ryan to make the voyage. Unlike brother Jack Walsh, who made his living traveling about, most Irishmen crossing the ocean did so only once. Michael was one of the rare ones who could afford a visit and he divided his time between Mary Ann's family in Brooklyn and Timothy's in Manhattan. Young Michael, Jack, Jerry and Ellen Walsh, ranging in age from six to two, ran around the third-floor apartment on Henry Street, vying for their grandfather's attention. Michael seemed happy telling them stories and walking them around the neighborhood.

For Mary Ann, her father's visit was an answer to her prayers. This was the opportunity for reconciliation with her family that she had so hoped for. Michael, for his part, opened himself with affection to this thirty-six-year-old daughter, the mother of four and ready to give birth to a fifth, who had suffered through the deaths of two children.

Michael brought news of the eight Ryan sisters and brothers in Ireland. John, just below Mary Ann in age, had entered the Trappist monastery of Roscrea in northern Tipperary, spending a good part of his time grinding flour for the community under the name of Brother Mecaire. The cloistered religious life was not unknown to the Ryan family. Michael's own brother had already spent almost forty years as a lay brother in the Trappist monastery of Mount Mellery in the mountains of County Waterford. Brother Bonaventure, as he was called, had been refused entrance twice before the Abbot finally decided to admit him. This Ryan had had a penchant for the bohemian life and enjoyed playing the fiddle in local pubs. His prior habits, however, proved no lasting impediment to the silent, rugged life he adopted at the isolated Trappist community.

A month after Michael's departure, Mary Walsh was born, in October of 1900. A girl baby might take the place of the one just lost.

But the enduring tragedy of the summer of 1900 continued because the source of dysentery remained unidentified. Patrick and Mary Ann were unknowing and undefended when the disease struck again during the July heat of 1901. As before, it attacked the youngest, the most vulnerable, and this time both little girls contracted it.

At first it was not evident how seriously ill the children were. Patrick had spent his day off at Mary Ann's side while she nursed the youngsters. The next morning he readied himself for work at Foley's

Bar. As he bent over the bed to say good-bye to the three-year-old Ellen, the child lifted both hands to his collar and held him. "I won't see you, Papa," she said. Startled, Patrick assured the feverish little girl that she would feel better soon and that he would come back very quickly if she needed him. But she stopped breathing so suddenly in the late afternoon that he never made it in time. When word reached him, he headed home for what became an unabated nightmare continuing over the next two weeks. Nine-month-old Mary died five days later. Two small white caskets followed one another through a wake in the family living room, down the flights of stairs and over the two blocks to the funeral mass at St. Charles.

Jere Cronin, a family friend and fellow parishioner who had an undertaking business around the corner on Atlantic Avenue, took care of the funeral arrangements. But the second casket was hardly buried when all three boys began to complain of the now-familiar deadly symptoms — Michael, seven; Jack, five; and Jerry, four.

Cursing the inept medical attention the children had been receiving, Jere Cronin abandoned his undertaking role to champion the cause of life. There was a certain Doctor Callen in the neighborhood, highly regarded for his medical skills but whom addiction to alcohol had made unreliable. Cronin said he thanked the saints in heaven that he found the doctor sober and rushed him to the third floor of 298 Henry. As the story is told, Callen claimed the first doctor had been starving the children — a totally wrong approach — and immediately initiated a new feeding schedule by administering to each boy a spoonful of brandy. They gained strength and recovered.

One can picture Patrick and Mary Ann kneeling together in St. Charles church, giving fervent thanks that their sons had been spared and pleading for strength to accept the terrible loss of their little girls. The only personal allusion to that period is in a stanza of a poem that Patrick wrote to Mary Ann some twenty years later on the occasion of their thirtieth wedding anniversary.

> With humble home you were content
> And felt that you were wealthy

When you could see sufficiently
The children strong and healthy.
You bravely met the Angel Death
Though sorely he did wound you.
Like Mother of the Machabees
As strong in faith he found you.
While others sank unto despair
You did not sit repining
In darkest cloud you did perceive
A rift of silver lining
Now in the evening of your life
What more could God have given
Than four angelic souls to meet you
At the Gate of Heaven

Son Paul, born five years after his sisters' deaths, remembered studying the suffering figures in the pictures that always hung side by side in his parents' bedroom — one of Jesus before Pilate and the other of the Sorrowful Mother. Patrick and Mary Ann had lost their eldest son and now all three daughters. But the three living sons who needed them were reason to carry on.

It was probably during that fall of 1901 that Patrick seriously entertained thoughts of returning to Ireland. He felt keen sympathy for Mary Ann who had spent ten years of marriage in almost constant pregnancy and childbirth. Rearing the children in such close quarters had been difficult. Losing four had been close to overwhelming. Back in Ireland she would at least have the emotional support of her large family.

Patrick had financial worries also and calculated how much less it would cost him to raise his family on a farm in Tipperary. Even the question of space must have stirred his thoughts in the direction of home. Living with several small children on one floor on a city street was a far cry from the open fields and meadows and the pure air of Ballydine. How much healthier for the children, he could reason, while his own heart longed for it also.

Tom Foley must have noticed Patrick's restlessness. As reliable a worker as Patrick had become, it was obvious that a bartender's life would not suit him in the long run. For one thing, this Irishman never drank and there were occasions when a bartender was expected to socialize and accept a drink offered by a regular customer. Foley encouraged Patrick to fraternize more, making himself better known to the Tammany Hall members who frequented the bar. One of these gentlemen caught sight of the bartender one day as he easily hoisted a large beer keg to his shoulder. "You'd be a fine candidate for the Fire Department, Paddy. Look into it; they're hiring able young men like you."

CHAPTER THREE

The Clang of Fire Bells

1901 - 1903

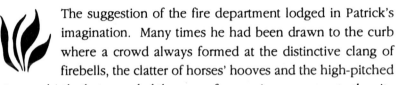The suggestion of the fire department lodged in Patrick's imagination. Many times he had been drawn to the curb where a crowd always formed at the distinctive clang of firebells, the clatter of horses' hooves and the high-pitched steam whistle that sounded the race of an engine company to the site of a fire. The air of urgency, excitement and danger, as well as the call to bravery that typified the fireman's job, held a peculiar attraction for Patrick. It was probably he who selected the poem that prefaced his first Annual Report as commissioner forty years later:

> His foe is fire, fire, fire!
> Bring him to the victor's car
> Richer is his spirit of war
> Than from Roman battle far
> Who has triumphed over fire.[1]

Patrick's move toward the city's fire department was not at all unusual. The Irish immigrant of the period commonly turned to the city bureaucracy for work, especially to the fire and police departments. No special experience was required for these departments and the selected candidates were trained on the job. The Irish immigrant did not face a language barrier, often measured up to the physical agility standards and found his imagination goaded by the daring aspects of a policeman's or fire fighter's work. If any political sponsorship was needed for entry into the fire department of 1901, Tom Foley readily supplied that for his bartender.

Up the Fire Department Ladder

Joined:	December 10, 1901
	(Engine Company 7)
School of Instruction:	January 11 - February 10, 1902
Fireman 4th Grade:	March 10, 1902
Fireman 3rd Grade:	March 10, 1903
Fireman 2nd Grade:	March 10, 1904
Fireman 1st Grade:	March 10, 1905
Engineer	April 2, 1905
	(Engine Company 21)
	April 1, 1906
	(Engine Company 7)
Lieutenant:	June 4, 1908
	(Engine Company 30)
Captain:	December 25, 1910
	(Engine Company 7)
Battalion Chief:	November 1, 1917
	(1st Battalion)
Deputy Chief:	May 16, 1925
	(11th Division)
Assistant Chief:	November 10, 1926
Acting Chief of Department:	February 23, 1940
Chief and Commissioner:	May 10, 1941
Retired:	January 1, 1946

But Patrick encountered an unexpected obstacle. He was by then thirty-three years old and the legal limit for admission into the department was twenty-nine. He visited his parish priest to discuss this — could he possibly tell a lie on his application? The advice of the clergyman was succinct and pragmatic: "State what you want and let the city investigate it." Patrick entered his age as twenty-eight and so was forced to be consistent in that five-year deduction for the next forty-four years. The man LaGuardia chose as commissioner in May of 1941 was not sixty-seven as the mayor thought, but seventy-two. Until the year of his death, Patrick's health and energy were such that no one doubted the accuracy of the date of birth entered on his city personnel record. Yet, his son Paul attests that his father was bothered throughout his life by this falsification of his age.

The firehouse where Patrick reported on December 10, 1901, was a shocking disappointment to the eager recruit. Headquarters for Engine Company 7 was 22 Chambers Street in City Hall Park, a structure razed a few years later* and already in dilapidated condition when Patrick reported there as a "proby."** Local sewers had been disconnected for the construction of the Lexington Avenue subway and a stench pervaded the area. The horse manure that accumulated in the basement of the firehouse added its own foul smells. Patrick could recall forty years later "the composite odor, not a reminder of Macy's perfume counter, made me impulsively grab my nose."[2]

Subway-related blasting easily shattered glass, so the windows at 22 Chambers were haphazardly covered with cardboard. Cracks and leaks abounded in walls and ceilings promising only minimal protection from cold and rain. And such was to be Patrick's home both day and night. The assignment of work shifts in the fire department is effected through a platoon system, and the "one-

---

* *Coincidentally, the Municipal Building (built 1909) where Patrick later had his office as Commissioner is constructed on this very site.*

** *A probationer or new fireman.*

platoon" system operative in 1901 continued for the next eighteen years. A fireman was on continuous duty for nine twenty-four-hour days, followed by the tenth day off. He slept at the firehouse and was relieved daily for three hours, one for each meal. From the start, Patrick began a practice that he continued during the many years that his company assignments were in lower Manhattan. If there were no fire calls at mealtimes, he walked over the Brooklyn Bridge and home to Brooklyn Heights for either lunch or dinner. He loved to cross the bridge at rapid gait and view the water traffic and skyline that he knew so well from his ferryman days. Entering his front door he greeted the family in Irish fashion, "God bless all here." They knew if he had come from a fire by the stench of smoke that clung to his clothing.

Scant knowledge and lack of concern for basic elements of fire safety in the construction of buildings turned a congested Lower Manhattan into a potential tinder box. There was constant action for the fire companies located south of 14th Street. One writer casts such action in the romantic glow of history:

> The steam fire engine with its three charging horses is a never-to-be-forgotten scene from the bygone days of city life. It is a picture out of the past, quite distinctively American, like the clipper ships, the stage coach, the prairie schooner, iron horse or Mississippi steamboat. It belongs to the smoky, bustling cities, the heavy-timbered red-brick factories and buildings, the dingy, gaslit streets of that industrious half-century between the Civil War and World War I.[3]

Horses played a central role in the daily routine of a firehouse in 1901. At Engine Company 7, seventeen horses were needed to pull the steam engine, the hose wagon, ladder truck, fuel wagon, chief's rig and spare apparatus. Feeding and caring for those animals was one of the time-consuming tasks of the firemen, especially the "probys." Besides the considerable quantity of hay and water distributed around, there were other jobs. Patrick remembered forty years later:

*1902. Fireman Walsh admiring Old Joe,
the pride of Engine Company 7, Chambers Street.
Note the dalmation on Old Joe's back.*

> My legs ache when I recall the hours of ceaseless pedaling on the bicycle that supplied the power for clipping the horses. Little sleep for the chambermaid to a gang of horses! The stalls needed continuous attention and it was not unusual to send a man to supper at 4 a.m.[4]

Horses were thoroughly trained to their job by selected firemen who applied great patience and method until the animals could respond with swiftness and accuracy to the sound of the fire alarm. Harnesses were kept suspended from the ceiling of the firehouse on an automatic hanger held in position by springs. The horses could move from their stalls into position in an instant. One tug of the reins and the harness dropped into place. Then, "a watchman snapped the collars fast . . . and the apparatus roared away as the members of the crew sprang to their places, donning their hats and coats en route. Everything was automatic except the movement of the horses from their stalls and the snapping of their collars."[5]

A fire horse was a very dedicated creature and it was always a sad event in any company when a veteran steed was forced to retire from duty at the first signs of slowing down. Though put out to pasture, the animal never lost his highly-trained instincts. Fire department records are full of instances in which some driverless milk wagon or garbage cart arrived at a fire. A retired horse who recognized his old outfit was near impossible to restrain.

In 1945, Commissioner Walsh reminisced about one famous horse in an article titled "Old Joe," published in the fire department magazine. It described a member of the horse team that pulled the steamer of Engine Company 7 at the turn of the century. Surely the most intelligent animal in the New York Fire Department, Old Joe had scores of admirers, including even the great prizefighter John L. Sullivan. "Shake hands, Joe," bellowed the visiting Sullivan, and Joe would offer his hoof for a vigorous pumping. When a chief visited quarters and the men of the company had to assemble on the apparatus floor, it was only necessary to say, "Call the men, Joe," and, with the bell rope between his teeth, Joe would ring until everybody came together. On one occasion this singular animal and his partner won a contest for speed against a number of competing horse teams. The time between the first stroke of the gong and the rolling of the apparatus was clocked at four and a half seconds. The tale of Joe, as recalled by the commissioner, was just slightly incredible. Surely the firemen reading it in the 1940's sensed this Irishman's native ability to weave a compelling story from a limited number of facts.[6]

In the days of the one-platoon system, a fireman's home was the firehouse where he lived for nine out of ten days. His family home was for visiting on the tenth day. In the normal routine of the nine days on duty, about seventy-five percent of that time was spent in the confines of the firehouse. The buildings — often Victorian style, heavy-walled and ornate — are still familiar landmarks on the streets of New York. On warm summer days the door were left open and firemen not engaged in assigned chores sat on benches outside. Cold weather meant long periods indoors. On the second level, above the apparatus floor, a game room adjacent to the sleeping quarters was the place where the men gathered to play billiards or pinochle. One writer paints a picture of life behind those Victorian doors in the early 1900's.

> . . . The atmosphere in the fire house was charged with a feeling of impending action. It seemed always that with every next tick of the clock the gongs were going to strike.
>
> During the long winter nights the big room (where the apparatus stood) echoed with the sound of the wind outside, the rattling of the big front doors . . . the occasional hoof thumps from the horses up back . . . the knocking together of billiard balls and the talk and laughter and footsteps resounding from upstairs.
>
> The main floor was dark save for a small lamp on the watch desk and the lantern that hung one on each side of the hose wagon, steam engine, ladder truck and chief's carriage. . . . There sat the man on watch at a tilttop desk on which the journal lay opened and ready to take the record of the next alarm. He

sat alone, the house rules keeping all the other firemen upstairs.
. . . Turned-down boots stood waiting in pairs in strategic places
about the floor, and rubber coats with the insides up so the
sleeve holes could be found in a hurry, hung conveniently over
knobby parts of the apparatus.

The yawning harness swinging over the front of each (piece
of apparatus), the ropes from the ceiling holding up the harnesses and the several brass sliding poles, all filled the room with
a forest of intricate gear . . . like the ropes and masts on the deck
of a ship.[7]

Although a company might go for stretches without a call, fire duty in
Lower Manhattan could be intensive. Patrick doubtlessly singled out
the most dramatic in his recollections forty years later of a fifty-two-
hour stint of unrelieved duty. It began at four a.m. on a Sunday with
a fire at an excelsior plant on Cooper Square that took twenty-one
hours to subdue. As the men reached home and were backing their
gear into the Chambers Street firehouse, another alarm sounded from
a box on Madison Street. One hour to help out there and then rush
to the assistance of another company at Spring and Mulberry. When
that scene was under control, a call came to reinforce yet another
company's efforts at a fire on the corner of Hester and the Bowery. It
was eight a.m. on Tuesday morning when a beleaguered crew arrived
back at quarters and was declared relieved of duty.*

Patrick's reminiscences never seemed to include the many frustrating false alarms. A tally of the time, money, injury and death to
firemen in the course of responding to false alarms has always been
scandalous and peculiarly tragic.

Another story Patrick liked to tell from his fledgling days oc-

---

* A complex charting system indicates which companies respond to fires
in a specific geographic area on a first, second, third, fourth and fifth
alarm, the alarms increasing with the extent of the fire. As companies
are directed on higher alarms to go to the aid of the first companies
called, still other companies must be on alert to back up depleted
manpower if fires erupt in their areas.

curred during a two-month stint of duty on Staten Island. New York City was establishing a branch of the regular fire department there to replace a volunteer force that had traditionally served Staten Island. Responding to a blaze in the B & O coal yard on Richmond Road, the new fire crew found that the only available hydrants were at the top of a hill too steep for the horses to climb. How could they get water to put out the fire and also douse the razzings of the unsympathetic volunteers who had turned out in number to watch the "pros" in action? After animated discussion the firemen stretched one hundred and fifty feet of hose from the hydrant to the steam engine positioned at the bottom of the hill. The intake valve showed a pressure of eighty-five pounds and the necessary water was released.

Patrick remembered relating this story many years later at an informal gathering which included several civil service examiners. To his surprise, the problem, shifted to Brooklyn, appeared on the next examination for battalion chief.

As with his recollections of the faithful horse Joe, Patrick also looked back nostalgically to the life of a fireman in the one-platoon system in effect for the first seventeen years of his career. He penned a simple rhyme, probably in the 1930's, drawing a larger than life picture of those earlier fire fighters:

> Indeed they were a rugged crowd
>   That never knew a fear;
> Though work was hard and hours long
>   Yet still they loved it dear;
> Were always ready for a fight
>   At midnight or at noon,
> There was no time for grumbling
>   There was but one platoon.
>
> Few of them could do square root
>   Or conjugate a verb
> Nor tell the species of a flower
>   That should be called an herb
> Of H^2O they never heard
>   Yet they could sing and croon,
> Direct a stream and swing an axe,

> Those men of one platoon.
> Inhalators or pulmotors
> Were never needed then;
> Were they knocked out, they took them out
> But soon went back again.
> Oh, give me back those good old days,
> To hear them sing and croon
> That happy band, who worked and sang,
> Who had but one platoon.

There is plenty of bravado in Patrick's jaunty verses. The shared life for long periods which characterized one platoon engendered an esprit de corps among the men that was hard to replicate when this basic pattern was altered. But that his men of one platoon never knew a fear is something he could hardly have meant seriously. "Home of the Bravest" is the caption spelled out in large letters over the entrance to the headquarters of the NYC Fire Department. But the brave are often fearful too. That the claim of the "bravest" is just can be known for sure only by those individuals who spend their days or their nights in readiness for the call of a fire. In 1908, the daring, popular chief Croker had worded it this way:

> Firemen are going to be killed right along. They know it, every man of them. . . . Firefighting is a hazardous occupation; it is dangerous on the face of it to tackle a burning building. The risks are plain. . . . Consequently, when a man becomes a fireman, his act of bravery has already been accomplished.[8]

Even for the most seasoned fire fighter who analyzes and prepares his strategies before entering a burning building, the number of unknowns is large and the risks enormous. A sudden shift of wind or the collapse of an interior wall can imprison a fire fighter who is left with minutes or seconds of breathing time to hope that an alert and resourceful team member can hack open a passageway to reach him. The interdependence of members of a fire company becomes so strong that the injury or death of a co-worker feels like the injury or loss of kin.

The dramatic 1991 film "Backdraft" swept crowds of moviegoers inside the most realistic, raging fires ever produced on screen. A contemporary novel written by a former New York City fireman captures the atmosphere of danger and of entrapment that is a constant possibility for any member of the force:

Steely looked at the top of the doorframe and saw through the blackness that the wood was beginning to glow. It would burn through soon. He must not stop trying, banging, jabbing, kicking at the wall. . . . Time. The time was running fast and against him.

He wanted to lie down, to close his burning eyes, but the thought came to him that if he was going to buy it here, he would buy it kicking all the way. He would not let the fire just consume him without some movement, some violent response, and so he banged (the stick) against the wall repeatedly, like a madman, splintering the wood as much as shattering the plaster. . . .

The heat was pressing down from above, the fire spreading across the ceiling.

It was then he heard the heavy thump, followed quickly by the cracking thump. Two extraordinary thumps and the wall came through. . . . He fell back. It was okay. He closed his eyes, and felt the natural eye water glaze over them like a cold wet rag. . . . He wasn't sure if he were conscious . . . he saw the fire flooding the ceiling from one end of the room to the other....He also knew he was being saved. A brother.[9]

Patrick was only four months into his fire department career in April, 1902, when the top uniformed officer, Edward Croker, was suspended from duty. Chief Croker was the nephew of Tammany Hall boss Richard Croker, who had resigned his leadership position after Tammany lost power in the city elections of 1901. The appointment of Edward Croker to a top fire department position had clearly stemmed from his uncle's influence. But Edward's tenure in office soon had the enthusiastic support of the department's rank and file. Croker was an extremely efficient fire fighter and he won the hearts of his men with his custom of plunging into danger spots with careless abandon. A colleague of Croker summed it up for the many:

"It steadies a young fireman to look around and see the Boss there." [10]

The new city administration, which took office in January of 1902, was soon at odds with the Tammany-appointed fire chief. Little time elapsed before Croker was charged with technical violations of regulations, was brought to trial and dismissed. But it was not in Edward Croker to give up after the first round. He went to court and waged a two-year legal fight for reinstatement. The fact that Tammany Hall returned to power in the 1903 city elections might have had some palpable effect on Edward Croker's court victory. He was reinstated as fire chief in February, 1904, to the general delight of the department, and continued at his post until his retirement in 1911. The novice fireman, Patrick Walsh, must have followed the high-echelon wrangling with lively interest and possibly chagrin. The message was that politics and the running of a fire department were hard to disentangle. Patrick must have been particularly happy to see Croker reinstated. The chief represented a brand of leadership the novice would try to imitate when his turn came around.

Sometime in 1903, one too many sticks of dynamite exploded underground during the Lexington Avenue subway construction. The 22 Chambers Street firehouse, already gravely shaken by these subterranean operations, was finally declared a dangerous environment for men, horses and apparatus alike. A brand new home for Engine Company 7 was already under construction on Duane Street and slated for opening in 1904. Clearly Company 7 could not hold out at 22 Chambers that long and managed to spend the interim at temporary quarters on neighboring Beekman Street.

CHAPTER FOUR

Up the Promotion Ladder

1903 - 1913

Patrick claimed he had not thought about promotion on the job until some friends who were studying for the Engineer's exam talked him into taking it with them.* Certainly the extra money would be welcome. There was a fourth son at home now — Joseph had been born in October, 1902. Because he lacked a full two years in the department by the fall of 1903, Patrick needed the Commissioner's approval to file for a promotional exam. That obtained, he and the other applicants were detailed for thirty days to the repair shops to study and work on every type of engine in use in the department.

Patrick's lifelong addiction to study probably got a major boost in this period. Since promotions were based on competitive civilservice examinations, his study habit helped to move him along. Dedication was essential if one planned to study amid the noise of billiard and pinochle games in the firehouse. When an exam was approaching, Patrick also studied on his treasured day off while Mary Ann occupied the children and tried to preserve for him a corner of the apartment with less noise and distraction.

Some of Patrick's fondest recollections of Ireland were the years spent with the schoolmaster who had encouraged his reading and eagerness for learning. As earlier he had delved into books about farming techniques, now he was fascinated with all material related to the art and science of fire fighting. His innate competitiveness also

---

* Engineer was the rank between fireman and lieutenant, now obsolete.

propelled him toward study. Years before he would not tolerate harvesting grain with a two horse-drawn reaper if a neighbor owned one with three. Now, if there were openings for promotion, he planned to contend for a high place on the list.

Even at the scene of a fire, Patrick very early gained a reputation for competitiveness. Fellow firemen from Company 7 remembered his jousting to be first inside a burning building. But he also extended this impulse to his company as a group in relation to other fire units. If the first alarm belonged to 7 and a second company was summoned to the fire as a back-up, woe to it if it arrived on the scene ahead of 7. One stanza in Patrick's "The Days of One Platoon" illustrates the point:

> Oh, how they loved to fight a fire
> They were a jealous band,
> Were they first due, a fire to lose
> They could not understand.
> It raised their ire to such a pitch
> A fire they prayed for soon
> To show the gang who stole their fire
> They were the best platoon.

The day before the written exam for Engineer was scheduled in January, 1904, a major blaze erupted at the Kips Bay Brewery at Manhattan's 39th Street and First Avenue. Company 7 responded on the fifth alarm at eight in the morning. In his capacity as "engineer-in-training" Patrick fed and nursed his engine at the scene of the fire for a straight twenty-four hours. Snow had developed in the afternoon and fell all that evening. Fireman Walsh was relieved at 8 a.m. the next day which left him two hours before the examination. According to Patrick, he actually fell asleep during the test until an unselfish brother poked him in the back. In spite of this lapse, he placed sixth on the civil service list, winning out over hundreds of older, more experienced men.

Just ten days after this Patrick was swept up in a historic event. The "Great Baltimore Fire" of 1904 figures as the first of the most famous or infamous conflagrations of the 20th Century. It almost

Engineer Walsh, on right, in 1906. He often spent hours stoking and nursing this engine at the scene of a fire.

razed Baltimore, destroying 2,500 structures on twenty miles of streets in an area of eight city blocks, and caused an estimated $125,000,000 in damages. The blaze broke out at eleven a.m. on February 7 and quickly outstripped the capacities of Baltimore's sixty-eight companies. An alarm was issued for emergency assistance from Washington, Wilmington and Philadelphia, and even these reinforcements were not enough.

At two a.m. on Sunday morning, February 8, Patrick Walsh was reading a book at the watch desk of Engine Company 7. The terse message he received was: "Proceed to the Liberty Street ferry forthwith." It was still too early for the morning papers with their vivid accounts of the disaster in Baltimore. One rumor among the men had it that the "City of Baltimore" ferryboat, docked in the Liberty Street slip, had caught fire. Another conjecture was that a fire had broken out in Baltimore & Ohio Railroad yards in Jersey City. To their surprise, the one hundred New Yorkers arriving in Jersey were loaded onto a train along with engines and equipment that filled nine flatbeds. Thirty-four horses rode in two stock cars. Some reporters at the station gave them news of the happenings in Baltimore and they learned that their own trip was the New York mayor's response to the disaster.

At 6:25 a.m. the trains rolled. Breakfast was a cup of coffee during a few minutes' break in Philadelphia. Frozen lines and track-switching caused long delays and the train took nine hours to reach Baltimore.

The scene of devastation that met the New York fire crew stayed with Patrick through his lifetime. And so did the following incident. A half hour after arrival in the city, the men had taken their assigned positions in an area of coal and lumber yards and had their engines in operation. But not a drop of water shot out at the blaze. A quick investigation revealed that the outlets on the Baltimore hydrants were one-quarter of an inch smaller than the connection carried on the New York apparatus. Had the trip been wasted? In frustration the men cast about for some way around the impasse. Finally Patrick slipped the large hose over the hydrant opening and bound the two together with a rope as tightly as he could. "Now try it," he shouted. Water gushed through the improvised hook-up and the steamer received enough for several powerful streams. "Why you blankety-blank so-and-so," said a colleague. "You'll be chief of the department some day."

Though the battle with the fire was exhausting, the trip home was a major ordeal. The train's steam connections were faulty and the cars had no heat. "It was the coldest trip we ever knew. We were frozen well nigh still and our horses were laid up," recalled Patrick.[1] A member of Engine Company 16 caught pneumonia and subsequently died. The contingent arrived back in New York at noon on Wednesday, three and a half days after the initial notice to move out.

Three months after the Baltimore expedition, Patrick was more witness than participant in a famous New York fire. The S.S. General Slocum was an excursion steamer chartered by the congregation of a German Luthern church. On the morning of June 15, 1904, it set out from a dock on the lower East River carrying 1,400 passengers bound for a picnic at Locust Point. As the boat passed Randall's Island opposite 125th Street, fire broke out in the cabin. When word reached him, Chief Croker sped uptown in his red auto, the first horseless vehicle in the department. Patrick's Engine Company 7 was one of those summoned to follow the chief uptown. Fully expecting the now blazing vessel to dock at the foot of 138th Street, the fire crew assembled there with apparatus. To their amazement and horror, the boat pressed on. For whatever reason, the captain did not halt the steamer until 149th Street, and on North Brother Island instead of the mainland. The scene by then was an inferno. The boat was beached in such a way that most of its length extended into deep water and many victims who escaped burning were drowned. River craft swarmed to the rescue but the worst had already happened. One thousand thirty-one of the 1,400 passengers were lost, more than half of them children. New York had never seen such a toll in human life from one fire disaster.

At the Walsh home on Henry Street another baby was born in November, 1904. To the parents, the event was a special gift since the baby was a girl. They baptized her Mary after her deceased sister and made a special plea to the Blessed Virgin for her continued health and safety.

A brand-new fireman, after completing a short course of instruction, was assigned the rank of Fireman 4th Grade. He automatically advanced a grade each successive year. In March, 1905, having reached the rank of Fireman 1st Grade, Patrick was finally eligible for the promotion that awaited him as a result of his score on the test of the year before. On April 2, 1905, he was appointed Engineer, with assignment to another company. Although pleased with his new status and salary increase, he reluctantly said good-bye to his friends and comrades of Company 7 and reported to Engine Company 21 located at 216 East 40th Street. For the first time he was moving away from Lower Manhattan, or the heart of the city, to the "outlying" area of uptown.

His isolation lasted only a year. Learning that an opening for engineer had developed in his old company, Patrick applied for a transfer back. In April, 1906, he rejoined 7, now installed in its new headquarters at 104 Duane Street. Eighty years later, Company 7 was still housed at the same location and shared its age-worn building with the Fire Department Museum.[2] The sleek, modern fire trucks parked in the left half of the building contrasted sharply with the collection of quaint old fire engines on display in the museum section to the right.

The structure itself appeared as interesting as the horse-drawn apparatus it housed. The interior gave the impression that very little had been done to it since its construction eighty years earlier. The narrow wooden stairs creaked from use; the high stamped-tin ceilings, but for a rare coat of paint, had not been touched for decades. An exhibit of old fire department photographs occupied the rather bare and dreary third floor, but imagination could conjure up the bunk beds lined side by side and the voices of the firemen of the early 1900's for whom these very walls had been home.

In June of 1906, Paul, the tenth and last baby, was born. By now the six surviving children chafed at the space limitations of their apartment. The older ones — now twelve, ten and nine — were constantly in each other's way. Patrick longed for a place other than the kitchen table for reading and studying. Mary Ann, whose daily life centered on home and children, must have suffered the close quarters most of all. After checking what available housing existed in the neighborhood, the couple decided to move no farther than across the street where they rented the brownstone house at the southeast corner of Henry and State Streets. Now they could expand to fill three floors.

Characteristic of such buildings, the high steps of 303 Henry led up to the front door and "parlor" floor. From the sidewalk it was a few steps down to the lower level while, above the parlor, were two additional floors. From the outset, Mary Ann subleased the four rooms on the top floor to outside tenants, screening for reliable, quiet types, usually single women or elderly men. Especially attractive was the ample yard at the rear of the house, completely walled in, with an entrance on the State Street side. A paved yard was a rare commodity in the neighborhood and made a fine playground for the children.

Although the kitchen and family room on the lowest level were the center of activity, it was the uniqueness of the parlor that Paul Walsh, as an adult, remembered most. It was always in perfect order, ready for visitors. The family used it themselves on holidays, birthdays and other special occasions. To the young boy, the room was dominated by the pictures on the walls, one of Mary Ann's parents, Michael and Catherine Ryan, and another of Patrick's father standing alone. In Paul's recollection, the pictures were four feet high by three feet wide and set in gold frames which needed to be gilded every few years. On the opposite wall was another four-foot frame containing a likeness of the boy Christ teaching the wise men in the temple.

A large, square-looking piano dominated the parlor and an overstuffed couch and several upholstered armchairs lined the walls. The first phonograph the family owned stood between the tall parlor windows. Paul recalled a few Al Jolson records in the collection, but his favorite was John McCormick singing "I Hear You Calling Me."

Why Patrick and Mary Ann never bought their own home, if not in 1906 at least at Patrick's promotions in 1908 or 1910, remains unknown. Paul suggests that Patrick did not want his money tied up in real estate, that he preferred a "pay as you go" approach that allowed cash for such expenses as tuition at Catholic schools. Patrick's daughter-in-law, Betty, felt that Patrick had an attitude toward renting in preference to owning, which was common among Irish immigrants. Most had never owned property in Ireland. Although the Walshes owned the house and farm in Ballydine, perhaps Patrick was reluctant to invest his personal time and money in the upkeep and repair of a Brooklyn home. Possibly, also, he and Mary Ann found it important to stay near St. Charles church, and houses in the area, even at that time, might have been beyond them financially. For whatever reason, the Walshes never owned their own home during the fifty years they lived in Brooklyn Heights.

The 303 Henry Street brownstone was home for the next ten years. Its enclosed yard became the hub of constant activity, generated by Michael, Jack and Jerry first, and later by Joseph, Mary and Paul. From his days of Irish football, Patrick loved sports and the challenge of physical activity and he encouraged his sons in whatever games interested them. Handball could be played against the brick wall of the neighbor's carriage house which formed part of the yard's enclosure. Michael set up a hoop for basketball and the father staked out a horseshoe area. Neighborhood boys always joined in and the yard became the local "hang-out." Mary Ann encouraged it. She liked the sound of young people's voices and tolerated the noise if it meant that her own boys were close to home. She evicted the last stragglers only when supper had to be started.

Some games called for more space and the older boys played them in the street. The superintendent of the building on the opposite corner of State Street was a crank who often chased youngsters away if their noise bothered him. One raucous stickball game on State Street brought an angry superintendent down to the sidewalks. At that same moment, the second-floor window flew open at 303 and Mary Ann thrust her head out to take up the defense of her boys. On Pop's day off, however, she was more sensitive to the noise and

The Walsh family, 1910. (Left to Right) Top: *Jack, Michael, Jerry.*
Seated: *Mary Ann, Joseph, Patrick.* Front: *Mary, Paul*

insisted that all activities be toned down. But Patrick's needs were not always predictable. Instead of resting when he arrived home, he sometimes dashed out the backdoor to join the youngsters in whatever game was in progress.

Michael, Jack and Jerry loved to organize neighborhood sports events. The passing traffic hardly bothered them when they dashed down Henry Street in a track or high-jump competition. As horses and carriages drove by, coachmen occasionally teased them by tickling their necks with the tip of a horse whip. When games finally outgrew the front street, the boys and their friends moved to the Parade Grounds at Prospect Park. And Michael rather grandiosely chose a name for them, "The American Athletic Association."

Around the corner from Henry Street, the foot of Atlantic Avenue runs down to the Brooklyn harbor and, in hot weather, Mike and Jack swam there, diving from the piers. Jerry never cared for swimming and kept his distance lest his brothers think to give him lessons by throwing him in.

Patrick and Mary Ann, always surrounded by children, developed the habit of calling each other "Pop" and "Mom." On occasion Mary Ann called him "Paddy," a derivation of the Gaelic for Patrick, "Padriac" or "noble." He never liked being called "Pat" or "Patty," the English derivatives. At times when Mom and Pop's points of view differed and an argument was brewing, Patrick would put his hands on her shoulders and say in jesting tone, "Now, listen, Mary Ann Ryan!" Usually that got them both laughing.

Although the backyard was largely concrete and meant to be trampled on, no one dared put foot on the minuscule front yard where Patrick encouraged a small hedge and patch of grass and, in early summer, added pansies and geraniums bought from a street vendor. It was a drop of country rescued from gray city pavements.

Nineteen hundred and seven was a historic year in New York's Fire Department when the first piece of horseless fire equipment was introduced on a trial basis. The force laughed at this "automobile fire engine," with its four-cylinder motor, that could sail down the street

Engine 30 as a triple company in 1909 at 278 Spring Street. Lieutenant Patrick Walsh is the third white hat from the left. (Today the building houses New York City's Fire Museum.)

at thirty miles an hour. Few thought it would ever challenge the horse's crucial role. A full nine years elapsed before the department, in 1916, seriously invested in motorized equipment.

In 1908 a promotional exam was held for the rank of Lieutenant, the next above Engineer, and Patrick scored high enough for an appointment. Once again, however, advancement meant a transfer away from Engine Company 7. Hoping that he would eventually work his way back as had happened before, he said his farewells to his friends and Lieutenant Walsh reported for duty at Company 30 located at 278 Spring Street.

The year 1908 saw a major breakthrough in fire-fighting capacity that far outshone the one self-propelled fire engine. New York City installed its first high-pressure water system in the area south of 23rd Street. The impetus for this measure had come from the fire insurance companies that were increasingly concerned about protecting their risks in congested, flammable districts. Their lobbying with the city administration finally brought about the installation of the new system. Now fire hoses connected to special pumping stations, water mains and safety hydrants could send high-pressured flows into the upper stories of the taller buildings.

A captain in the fire department is indeed "top dog" — feudal lord in his little kingdom. The firehouse contains a tightly-knit working force and a captain gives the orders and sets the tone. It is up to him to rally the spirits of his crew and make them into an efficient fire-fighting unit. As Lieutenant in Company 30, Patrick got back into his routine of study in off hours at the Spring Street firehouse. When the Captain's Exam was announced, he took and passed it. His appointment as Captain on December 25, 1910, was a Christmas present for himself and his family. And it was indeed a happy New Year when, on January 1, 1911, he was given the post of Captain at Engine Company 7, 104 Duane Street. Now he was returning to head the unit he had joined as a raw recruit nine years earlier. It consisted of three lieutenants, four engineers, twenty-three firemen, two horse-drawn engines and two hose wagons.

The man who returned to Company 7 in 1911 had physically

changed. He was forty-two years old and the barrel chest of the Tipperary farm boy was now more pronounced and muscular on his modest five-foot-six and three-quarter-inch frame. The oval face, with its high forehead, had accumulated lines in the intervening years and the dark, intense eyes were now highlighted by the black stem moustache.

When Patrick was appointed Commissioner by Mayor LaGuardia in May of 1941, several commentators mentioned that the mayor's decision was applauded by the rank and file in the department. This rapport with the firemen most likely had its roots in the season Patrick spent as captain at Company 7, between 1911 and 1917. Nine years of prior fire-fighting experience, almost exclusively in Lower Manhattan, had fed his prodigious memory with abundant data about buildings and lots, traffic flow and blockages that made up the checkered hodgepodge of the busiest section of New York City. This power of observation coupled with a native inventiveness when confronted with practical problems, had contributed to his growing skill as a fire fighter. His readiness to plunge ahead of his men into a burning building earned him their trust and admiration.

Thirty years later Patrick would maintain that the most tragic fire of his whole career was the one they were summoned to on March 25, 1911, at the infamous Triangle Shirt Waist Company. The factory employed six hundred thirty-five people in its sweatshops on the three top floors of the ten-story Asch Building at 23 Washington Place, off Washington Square Park. It was just fifteen minutes before closing time when two boys noticed a flame darting out of a rag bin on the eighth floor and attempted to douse it with pails of water. But the flames shot up and ignited layers of muslim and tissue paper lying on a nearby table. A standpipe hose stood in the corner, but when a man grabbed for it, it proved useless, rotted at the folds. Then began the stampede of employees down narrow aisles toward a single stairway exit and one slow-moving elevator. Mass hysteria spread to the ninth and tenth floors as well, as smoke and flames quickly rose toward the roof. Under the circumstances it was amazing that nearly five hundred workers escaped alive. Some made it across on the rooftop to the neighboring New York University Law School. But one hundred and forty-seven persons, the majority young girls employed as seamstresses, were burned to death within the building, or jumped from window ledges as flaming torches, to hit the pavement a hundred feet below.

It was soon a five-alarm fire and Patrick's was one of the numerous companies summoned to the scene. Although he arrived among the first, the situation was already beyond hope of early control. The apparatus had to be moved in cautiously to avoid crushing the bodies of girls who had already hurtled to the street. Worse than the screaming and shouting were the terrible thuds of the bodies that continued to hit the ground. "You should thank the Holy Mother you didn't see it," he would tell people years later, "so very sad it was." Bodies of the victims were taken to an improvised morgue at the East 26th Street Pier in the same wooden caskets that the victims of the General Slocum disaster had occupied seven years earlier.

New Yorkers responded with outrage to news of the Triangle Shirt holocaust. Public clamor for stricter building codes brought some significant results. The State Legislature passed a law requiring adequate exits, automatic sprinklers, fire escapes and limitations on occupancy. Jurisdiction for enforcement of these regulations were placed with a newly-formed section in the department — the Bureau of Fire Prevention. One of the early convictions under the new building code defied belief. A former proprietor of the defunct Triangle Shirt Waist Company was found guilty of keeping factory doors locked during working hours at his new company.

When the term "famous" is attached to a fire, it is bound to connote "infamy," in the sense of disaster, tragedy, loss of life and property. It was surprising that, less than a year after the Triangle Shirt Waist episode, another celebrated fire entered the history books. At five a.m. on January 9, 1912, flames were sighted leaping up inside the empty office building belonging to the Equitable Life Insurance Company between Broadway and Nassau Streets in Lower Manhattan. Had the fire broken out a few hours later, the building and surrounding streets would have been crowded with working people. Captain Patrick Walsh responded with his company on the first alarm. By the time the blaze was subdued four hours later, it had assumed five-alarm proportions and forty-one companies had been called in to fight it.

Six firemen lost their lives in the Equitable Building and among these was a battalion chief named William Walsh. Patrick rushed to a phone at the earliest opportunity to assure Mary Ann that he was not the Walsh who had died. His call succeeded in sparing her a great deal of grief, because, as so often occurs in a time of crisis, names are confused and word got out that Patrick Walsh had been lost. Mary Ann spent a good part of the day correcting the rumor as friends and neighbors called to extend their condolences.

While the fire was raging that wintry January morning, the temperature dropped sharply and the wind velocity increased. The volume of water directed at the burning building began to freeze on the outer walls, forming exotic patterns of thousands of icicles. Low temperatures persisted and, for many days after, this glacier-like mass of bizarre design attracted crowds of onlookers.

One positive response to the loss of life in the Equitable Building fire of 1912 was that, for the first time, fireproof construction materials became a subject of serious scientific research.[3]

While Captain at Company 7, Patrick was awarded the Bonner Medal, one of the highest decorations in the department. He earned it on June 14, 1913, when the company was summoned on a fifth alarm to a storage lot at Rutgers and Water Streets where several hundred barrels of gasoline had caught fire. The flames were finally extinguished and the men started rolling the untouched barrels into the street out of danger. But a new spark was created, perhaps even by someone's shoe hitting the cement sidewalk, and instantly the scene was ablaze once again. Lieutenant Harry Schoener of Engine Company 15 was standing in the middle of the lot when all re-ignited and sheets of fire enveloped him from head to foot. The moment he fell, Patrick rushed into the flames, got a grip on Schoener, and managed to yank him across the lot and out of the debris. With help from other firemen, he extinguished the fire burning the man's clothes. Patrick ignored his own superficial scars and resumed his duties. Tanks continued to explode in all parts of the lot. It took hours to subdue the flames since the tremendous heat generated by burning oil was melting the hose at the hydrant. Lieutenant Schoener lay in a hospital for months, badly burned, but eventually returned to the force and, in later years, became a battalion chief in The Bronx.

There were other instances in Patrick's career when he responded bravely to emergency circumstances. Although he never missed an opportunity to submit the accounts of outstanding performances on the part of his men, he was reluctant to report his own deeds. When chided about this by his co-workers, he'd reply, "What good are medals? You can't wear them to a fire, can you?"

Tammany lost the election of November, 1913, and the reformist John Purroy Mitchell became mayor. He appointed Fire Commissioner Adamson, who moved to reduce department expenditures by weeding out the Tammany practice of padding payrolls with nonfunctioning individuals. These measures reportedly caused a general uplift in the morale of the department's rank and file.

CHAPTER FIVE

To Raise a Family in Brooklyn
1913 - 1916

 At home on Henry Street the children were growing and the footsteps were heavier up and down the tall staircases. Paul, at five or six, had taken to sliding down the long, shiny bannisters. Each child, in turn, attended the parochial school just two blocks away at St. Charles. When it came time for high school for the older boys, Patrick and Mary Ann insisted that it be Catholic. Despite the influx around them of immigrants of all creeds and ethnic backgrounds, the couple believed they had uprooted themselves from Catholic Ireland and settled in Protestant America. The faith they might have taken for granted at home became a precious and delicate possession in the new environment, one that had to be constantly guarded and nourished. They viewed the Catholic school as the prime instrument for preserving the faith and the public school as the great leveler that would provoke religious doubts in immature minds.

Patrick also subscribed to the atmosphere of discipline that typified the Catholic school. He particularly liked the strict Franciscan Brother who was teacher to Michael in the seven grade at St. Charles. Michael, on the other hand, was glad to finish out that year and leave the grade and brother behind him. During the summer, Patrick learned that the brother in question had been transferred to the neighboring school of St. Paul and assigned to the eighth grade. Imagine Michael's dismay when his father decided to transfer him to St. Paul's so that he could have one more year with the imposing Franciscan.

Michael managed to survive under his dour instructor and, after graduation, entered St. James Academy on Jay Street in Brooklyn, taught by another order, the Christian Brothers. By the time Michael was a senior, Jack was in the same school as a sophomore and Jerry as a freshman. Private high school meant tuition, and all the economies Patrick and Mary Ann could devise were aimed at affording it. Years later, when Patrick was an assistant chief of department, a case of embezzled funds was investigated and the personal finances of fire department officials were reviewed as part of the proceedings. When the investigators inquired into the holdings of Patrick Walsh, he appeared with a bank statement showing a very modest savings account. "Gentlemen," said Walsh to the questioning faces, "my bank books are all at school."

Thriftiness was part of the fabric of life on Henry Street. Every light had to be extinguished when not in use. When a telephone was installed, only brief conversations were tolerated. Having learned how to cut the hair of his fellow firemen at the firehouse, Patrick now gave his boys their regular haircuts at an improvised barber shop in the family kitchen.

Between 1912 and 1915, when homes on Brooklyn Heights were being gutted or torn down to make way for the first apartment houses, Patrick hired a horse and wagon on several occasions and the boys loaded it with cast-off wood of every description to carry home and pile in their own backyard. This was burned in the furnace to save on coal. But the wood had not necessarily finished its service when reduced to ashes in the family furnace. Patrick supervised the sifting of these ashes to save the "clinkers" or chunks of wood that failed to burn the first time round and could be thrown in again. In the fall of the year, he inspected all the rooms in the house, stuffing rags into any cracks that might let in cold air.

As the boys approached their teens, they were all encouraged to find part-time jobs — shoveling snow for the homeowners on Brooklyn Heights, delivering groceries for the stores along Atlantic Avenue, adopting newspaper routes and latching on to sundry other seasonal odd jobs.

Paul remembered those summers when his father took regular

trips out to Long Island in a Lieutenant Smith's old jalopy to buy a supply of fresh vegetables in season at local farms. Mary Ann would cook, can and store them for the following winter.

Although Mary Ann readily went along with Patrick's economies, they did not hinder her generous bent. Any beggar who appeared at her door would be offered a cup of coffee and a sandwich or soup. But she was genuinely irritated one day on discovering that a visiting tramp had walked off with her cup and saucer.

It was hard for some to guess if Patrick's first love was his family or the fire department, but those who knew him best vouched for his family. When his day off was not occupied with domestic chores or study for an exam, he chose to spend it with his children. Since he loved the outdoors, he generally took them on some kind of excursion. What he did for the older three he repeated some five years later for the younger three. One favorite destination was Prospect Park in Brooklyn. Often they wound up at the Parade Grounds where the children played their own ball game in the side lot while Patrick climbed to a berth on the limb of a tree and watched an adult's baseball game in session.

On occasion they took a picnic to what was then called Celtic Park, a playing field bordering Calvary Cemetery in Queens, where Irish football or hurling was popular. One day the kickoff was followed by a fight between the contending teams of Irishmen which ended the football game before it actually began.

Another favorite outing on Sunday afternoons was a train ride over the Brooklyn Bridge and a walk down to Wall Street where Patrick and the children strolled up and down the empty blocks of the financial district. Perhaps Patrick associated the tall buildings and dark, canyon-like streets with Sunday solemnity. Weary feet finally got a rest at the Automat where all were treated to hot coffee.

Mary Ann joined the excursion if it were other than hiking. She particularly enjoyed the summer ferry rides. It was a special pleasure on a hot day to board the ferry that departed from the end of Atlantic Avenue and ride it to Battery Park at the tip of Manhattan. There they walked to an adjoining dock and caught a second ferry to Staten

Island. Each ride was five cents. They picnicked as the vessel chugged along and, on Sundays, the Staten Island line featured a group of musicians performing a brief concert on stringed instruments.

Occasionally, the family took day-long boat trips which they considered a real summer vacation. Excursions operated from lower Manhattan in several directions — around the curve of Brooklyn to Coney Island or, farther on, to Rockaway Beach; up the Hudson to Bear Mountain; and down and across greater New York Bay to Atlantic Highlands, New Jersey. Patrick, the former ferryman, never lost his taste for the swaying vessel, sea breezes, salt air and the vistas of a changing New York skyline.

Although time off from work was limited and the family engrossing, Patrick and Mary Ann were always interested in keeping contact with the close relatives who had immigrated to New York. There was Patrick's sister Bridget married to Mary Ann's brother Timothy Ryan, another sister, Anna married to Edward Maher and living in Flatbush, Brooklyn. The Ryans had seven children and the Mahers four. Many Ann's uncle on her mother's O'Brien side had also immigrated with his family. As the network grew, Mary Ann organized a cousins' reunion on a monthly basis. Paul Walsh remembered such gatherings in the parlor at 303 Henry Street when the rug was pushed back and thirty or more people danced the Virginia Reel. Regular get-togethers continued right up to World War I.

Some days when Patrick was on duty, Mary Ann took her troop of youngsters on the subway over to her brother Timothy's on West 18th Street in Manhattan. The older boys loved to take turns rapping the blacksmith's anvil. On one occasion Tim Ryan figured he would profit by the boys' keen interest and let them carry on while he took a break at the local pub. Minutes later, as Bridget was chatting with Mary Ann in the kitchen, she suddenly paused and seemed to cock one ear. "That's not Tim's stroke," she said. The unfamiliar rhythms had lasted a mite too long.

Although as a fire fighter and company commander the captain of Engine 7 was certainly orthodox, in other ways he was cut of a different cloth. On the one hand, the burly Irishman who never lost his thick brogue was active, outgoing and sociable. When a handball court was staked out in the small yard behind 104 Duane Street, the captain soon became the most enthusiastic and faithful of players. Days when fire duty was slack, he punctuated his working hours with six energetic games. His hapless partner soon realized that he had to play fiercely because Patrick was as seriously competitive in handball as he was in attacking fires.

Contrasted to Patrick's vigorous, volatile side was his meditative, philosophical streak rooted, first of all, in a deep religious faith. Once his work schedule became such that he was no longer on regular duty in the early morning, he attended daily Mass at St. Charles before reporting to the firehouse. He closely followed the text of the Latin Mass with his English missal, entering as fully as he could into the meaning of the ritual.

Patrick had a fondness for reading and much of what he devoured was religious in nature. Starting about 1915, he systematically covered the complete Bible every year and could impress Protestant and Jewish acquaintances with his knowledge of scripture. He reread the New Testament three times yearly and did the same with the devotional *Imitation of Christ* by Thomas a Kempis. He studied Catholic philosophy principally by following the best-known Catholic periodicals of that time: *America, Commonweal, The Catholic World, The Tablet, The Sunday Visitor.* Radio's Sunday evening "Catholic Hour" featured speakers such as Monsignor Fulton Sheen, Father James Gillis and Ignatius Smith, O.P., whom Patrick considered to be first-rate Catholic thinkers. On Monday mornings he would buy all the New York newspapers to peruse for their scriptural content the texts of Sunday sermons preached by noted Protestant ministers.

Patrick did some limited reading of classic English literature and his fondness for poetry led him to commit his favorite works to memory. He could recite the first four hundred lines of Longfellow's "Evangeline" without pause. At family supper one evening one of his sons, a high school freshman, was bemoaning the fact that he had to memorize ten lines of Scott's "Lady of the Lake." Patrick winked across the table to his wife and began to recite the first few stanzas of the poem. Mary Ann took the cue and recited the next few, and so on. That was the last complaint from the high school freshman. Mary Ann might have been recalling the poetry she memorized as a young girl while walking the mile from her family home in Ballydine to the country schoolhouse. Maybe she re-read favorite poems while sitting in the kitchen rocking chair in that single evening hour between the final noises of children and her own bedtime.

Probably the most unorthodox of Patrick's attributes was his penchant for writing poetry himself. Rather than conceal this habit around Engine Company 7, he flaunted it. At first his mates teased him but gradually they took it in stride and even began to encourage him. Patrick had the rare knack, admired by his fellows, of being able to jot out a few stanzas on practically any topic on a moment's notice. He wrote his poems on slips of paper, committed them to memory, and discarded the written scraps. Some colleagues began to retrieve these manuscripts as possible collector's items, should Patrick Walsh ever become a recognized poet. The quality of the poetry indicates why that never happened. Yet the man clearly revealed himself emotionally in his verses and, though sentimental, their innate fervor has its own appeal. On an evening in 1914 he stood on the shore of Brooklyn Heights watching the ceremony and celebration as President Wilson, at the foot of the Statue of Liberty turned a switch that for the first time threw electric light upon the tall lady. Patrick, thrilled at the occasion, went home to write:

> Miss Liberty, you looked so bright,
> I hardly knew you, when one night,
> 'Mid falling fire and cannon roar,
> I watched you from the Brooklyn shore.
> And many there were, that came to see,
> A few of whom were just like me.
> Who once a stranger, and alone
> You gladly welcomed to your home.

Oh! how can I forget that night
When from the ship I saw your light.
My heart was torn with grief and woe,
Because I knew not where to go.
Of my ancestors, none before
Sought refuge on your fertile shore.
So when I came, as you may see,
I sought but you, Miss Liberty!
Long may you shine, that you may be
To others as you were to me,
A guiding light, of hope and love.
And if that day should ever come
That foreign foe invade your home,

I hope and pray that I might be
The first to die defending thee.

This particular poem, like several others, brims with patriotic sentiment. As an immigrant who had finally found his niche, Patrick felt a sincere and abiding gratitude toward his adopted country. At a time when Catholics, in a predominantly Protestant land, were still suspect for their commitment to a Pontiff seated in Rome, the immigrant church also wished to prove that its members were as wholeheartedly American as their Protestant neighbors. God and country became a twin banner of allegiance. For Patrick who worked within a branch of secular government, the "God and Country" theme was especially relevant. Living in America through the waging of two World Wars only caused him to emphasize it.

In 1916 the landlord at 303 Henry Street raised the rent the Walshes were paying from seventy-five to one hundred dollars a month. Patrick and Mary Ann thought such a hike outrageous and set about looking for another suitable house in Brooklyn Heights. They finally settled for a structure just two and a half blocks away, at 155 State Street. It belonged to a row of three-storied sandstone houses constructed before the Civil War and continued in use since that time. Number 155 was first listed in the New York City Street Directory of 1856.

As before, the family rented the whole house. Patrick saw no need for hiring a moving van when he himself had a houseful of sons to do the job. Michael was already twenty-two, nearing completion of his studies at Fordham Law School. Jack was twenty-one and enrolled at St. Francis College. Jerry, at nineteen, was working at a local job. He had conducted his private war of independence from his father by refusing to consider a college education following his graduation from St. James Academy. Young Joseph, at fourteen, was well able to pitch in with the job at hand. Patrick rented a horse and wagon for ten dollars a day and the boys moved all the heavy furniture down the steep stairs on Henry Street and up the equally steep ones on State Street. Ironically, they had hardly moved in and settled when the new landlord advised that their rent was soon to be raised to one hundred dollars.

CHAPTER SIX

A Patriot Poet

1916 - 1920

Before the change in address, Michael began bringing a girl friend to the house. He had known Catherine Dundon since grammar school at St. Charles Borromeo. Although boys and girls were taught in separate buildings, the two had met at a parish dance. As Jack and Jerry also became interested in girls, the parents encouraged them to bring their dates home, especially for what became at 155 State Street the weekly family card game of "Setback," (which in some areas is referred to as "Pitch"). Patrick started keeping the scores on a pad that he filled with his heavy round numbers — one of an eventual pile of notebooks recording the scores over thirty years. He usually chose one of the younger children as a partner and together they "defended the house." Card playing did not interest Mary Ann. She spent the time preparing food in the kitchen and no one could leave until a meal had been served. Of all the card players, Patrick was the loudest and most enthusiastic. "An ace is always good for two" was one of his pronouncements. Pity the poor partner who failed to bid when Patrick held the right cards!

But all normal routines were suspended on April 6, 1917, when the United States declared war on Germany and officially entered the Great War that had been expanding in Europe since 1914. Jerry had received a month's training at sea in the Naval Reserve Force the year before and was now called into active duty. Michael finished Fordham Law School in June and could enlist in the Navy as a chief petty officer.

Jack graduated from St. Francis College in June. His weak eyes

A proud patriot, 1918. Battalion Chief Walsh with son Michael, LEFT, U.S. Navy Ensign, and son Jerry, RIGHT, Seaman.

would have kept him out of the armed services in any case, but he never entertained thoughts of enlisting. This son had already decided to enter a religious order and become a priest. One friend remembers Jack's consulting the membership rolls of the various congregations. The Franciscans and Redemptorists listed name after name of German extraction while the Dominicans appeared to be overwhelmingly Irish. Whether or not ethnicity was a deciding factor for Jack, in August, 1917, at age twenty-one, he entered the novitiate of the Dominican Order in Somerset, Ohio.

Within the space of a few months, the three oldest boys had left home, gone to serve God and country. Though they were putting into practice lessons learned at their parents' knees, Patrick and Mary Ann missed them keenly.

The United States' entry into the World War fanned Patrick's patriotism. It inspired the composition of a poem entitled "Old Glory" which he recited easily and often. Although exalted in style and sentiment, it is probably the best of his poetic attempts.

> Come fling Old Glory to the breeze
> And let it wave 'til air and seas
> Are from those monsters free,
> Who dare to take a gallant life,
> Unconscious of this bloody strife,
> While resting peacefully . . .

> To us who found asylum here,
> Is dear Old Glory doubly dear;
> And swear again, we do,
> That fatherland or motherland
> Between us now no more can stand
> We owe our all to you.

> For when you took us to your breast
> To make us free who were oppressed,
> When you could us exclude,
> What cowardly vipers we should be
> To dare betray such chivalry
> By base ingratitude.

But now we stand with all our might
Behind Old Glory in this fight,
A fight to keep us free,
And leave to children true and brave
What human hearts must ever crave
Justice and liberty.

When from our people we shall hear
A shout of triumph loud and clear
Burst forth from shore to shore,
When calm and peaceful all may sleep
Within the air and on the deep,
When war shall be no more,

When traitors from our shores are hurled
Then dear Old Glory shall be furled
Forever to remain
To those who fear not and are just,
Whose motto is, "In God We Trust,"
An emblem without stain.*

With patriotism running so deep in the household, Paul Walsh, age eleven, was not content with putting a flag out each morning and taking it in at dusk. Besides the one above the front door, he installed other flags on the two floors above. A square banner was hung inside the large parlor windows, a red border encompassing two blue stars against a white background.

For Jack in the seminary there were no trips home, but the Order permitted occasional parental visits. Ohio was very far from Brooklyn, but Patrick decided it would be a great treat for Mary Ann to make the train trip. He himself could not get away from his fire duties, particularly in wartime. Mary Ann had never enjoyed a real break from the everyday chores of house and family since her marriage. At this time she was especially worried about Michael and

---

* On the occasion of the dinner for his fortieth anniversary in the fire department in 1941, Patrick recited the full eight stanzas of the poem which the New York Herald Tribune printed the following day.

Jerry serving in the Navy. So, with assurances from thirteen-year-old Mary that she could manage the cooking for five days, the mother packed her suitcase and was given a warm send-off at Pennsylvania Station. Mother and son long remembered that visit. Jack, the delicate child, had always been close to his mother. He had missed his family very much during the first six months of separation and now he was delighted to have his mother nearby to visit for three consecutive days. They comforted each other in parting with reminders that, after Jack completed his year in Ohio, he would continue training in Washington, D.C., much closer to home.

With the older three away, the younger children were able to take center stage. The pattern had not changed much. Joe, and gradually Paul, looked for part-time work. One job roused them from bed early in the morning to turn off the gaslights, one by one, that lined the streets of the neighborhood. Each evening they walked the same route, turning lights on again.

Each in turn had the job of going from door to door selling the newspaper, *The Sunday Visitor*, at one cent a copy. Patrick had thought up this enterprise for reasons of faith rather than profit. Numerous Irish immigrant girls worked as servants in the wealthy homes on Brooklyn Heights. The more prosperous families employed several: a cook, upstairs maid, governess, laundress, attendant to the mother, and so forth. Servants were often on duty at seven in the morning, seven days a week. Patrick was concerned about the faith of these girls and felt they would be helped by reading the articles on religious doctrine in *The Sunday Visitor*. Paul remembers how he would stand at the partially open door while the maid went for her penny and he maneuvered to get a glimpse of the elegant furnishings inside.

Joseph had a fine record at St. Francis Prep on Butler Street and graduated at the age of fifteen. He would later complete St. Francis College at nineteen, Fordham Law School at twenty-two and be a practicing attorney at twenty-three. All the while he kept up some kind of part-time job to help pay his tuition costs.

Mary Florence, the only girl among five brothers, became a

tomboy. She played games hard and delighted beating neighborhood boys in local roller-skating contests. Paul, her junior by two years, remembers how Mary used to take the "long route" home from school. She had a penchant for running up the steep stairs of a brownstone house, jumping over the bannister to the pavement below and heading straight for the stairs next door. She clocked herself on how long it would take to get through a block in this fashion. By the time Mary started high school and the daily commute to Our Lady of Wisdom Academy in Ozone Park, she was making an effort to "act as a young lady," as she had been counseled. But she never was convinced by the pious adage "A whistling girl makes the Blessed Mother cry" and continued to whistle whenever she liked.

The war was in the forefront of everyone's mind. Michael spent most of his navy time in training and made his longest voyage aboard an oil transport running from Bayonne, New Jersey, to Galveston, Texas. His achievement was his ensign's commission in the Transport Service before the war's end — a final diploma capping a short-lived and rather eventless naval career.

Jerry, on the other hand, was a seaman assigned to the troopship *George Washington* and, during his two and a half years in active service, crossed the Atlantic forty times, very often in danger of submarine attack. The young seaman kept a diary on several of these trans-Atlantic trips. After the Armistice, the *George Washington* had the special honor in December, 1918, of carrying President Woodrow Wilson and his party to the peace conference in Versailles. "In less than a week, the *George Washington* was converted from a transport to a floating palace," wrote Jerry in his diary.

Wilson returned to France on the *George Washington* for a continuation of the peace conference in March, 1919. Jerry spent three months with the crew aboard the ship docked in the harbor at Brest, until word came on June 28 that the peace treaty had been signed and World War I was officially over.

"There was great rejoicing in the city. The forts and several ships fired the National Salute of twenty-one guns, while the remaining ships blew their sirens and whistles. Until midnight all the ships

*President Wilson reviews the Navy crew of the
George Washington en route to the signing of the
Treaty of Versailles, 1919. Jerry Walsh, LEFT, crossed the
Atlantic forty times during World War I.*

in the harbor were lit up like Christmas trees," Jerry recorded.

On the return crossing, the President's Fourth of July address to crew and troops was transmitted to Washington, D.C, by "wireless" telephone. On July 8 the *George Washington* approached New York harbor and thirty-three ships welcomed it near the Rockaways. Eight airplanes and a balloon took off from Sandy Hook, New Jersey, to accompany the President into harbor. Jerry had often seen Wilson close-up and several official photos were taken of Wilson with Jerry standing at attention at his side. "One thing I have to say about the President," wrote the young sailor, "he is the most democratic man I have ever met. Wherever you see him, you find him wearing that smile that makes those near him feel happy."

In October, 1919, when King Albert of Belgium sailed to America on the *George Washington* with his Queen and the young Prince Leopold, Jerry was appointed their official orderly. In a snapshot that survives, King Albert is seen standing informally on deck in shirtsleeves and suspenders while Jerry stands to one side at ease, chatting with another sailor.

During the return voyage of the royal family, Jerry carried the cake into the dining room for the Prince's sixteenth birthday. Whatever the modest services performed for the royalty by their orderly, he was honored by the Belgian monarch with the Silver Medal of Leopold II. Jerry records that it was conferred on him on November 12, 1919, at eleven a.m.

On another occasion the *George Washington* carried over the Atlantic the gregarious Assistant Secretary of the Navy Franklin D. Roosevelt. The *George Washington's* commanding officer was taken aback one day on entering Mr. Roosevelt's quarters and finding his orderly relaxing in a chair with the Secretary, both smoking big cigars. "This is my guest, Jerry Walsh," explained Roosevelt.

All during the war Patrick had followed the movie newsreels very closely to catch a glimpse of his son in the entourage of some important official on the deck on the *George Washington.* Jerry's siblings laughed at the irony of their sailor brother who constantly rode the high seas, although he was the only member of the family who had never learned to swim.

Following his discharge from the Navy in November, 1919, Jerry wrote *"A Short Synopsis of My Naval Career,"* covering seven type-written pages. It is the account of a youthful and enthusiastic partici-pant in a dangerous and thrilling operation. The text is quite literate and readable for a young man whose formal education had ended with high school.

Jerry's wartime experience aboard the *George Washington* may have been, in one sense, his finest hour. He probably thought of it often himself, recalling this season in his life when his father had truly been proud of him.

In November, 1917, Patrick took another career step. At age forty-nine he was appointed Battalion Chief in charge of New York City's 1st Battalion, with headquarters at 193 Fulton Street. Seven battalions had been established by then south of 23th Street, each overseeing five or six engine and one or two hook-and-ladder com-panies.* The battalion chief attended every first-alarm fire in his district.

This promotion for Patrick meant a final farewell to Engine Company 7. More than twelve of his sixteen years with the depart-ment had been spent with the men of 7, including his first year as probationer and his last years as captain. His hymn to the "days of one platoon" and "the rugged crowd that never knew fear" had been wholly dedicated to his friends and colleagues of Company 7.

By 1917 the New York City Fire Department was on its way to complete motorization. Only 700 horses remained in service and their average age was over thirteen. Firemen might have laughed in 1907 when the first "automobile fire engine" was introduced to the force on a trial basis, but nine years later the commissioner had called for a million-dollar appropriation for motorized equipment. The

---

* *The role of the hook-and-ladder company is to open up the building, permitting smoke to escape and clearing a path for the engine company's hoses.*

dramatic scene of galloping horses drawing the fire engine behind them was becoming a rarity on the city's streets. By 1922 the last of the "Old Joe's" had retired, leaving only nostalgic recollections of a more colorful era.

The aura surrounding the "spirit of one platoon" was rapidly fading also as firemen became identified with the movement toward improved working conditions that workers all over the country shared. In 1919 the two-platoon system was officially adopted. Under "two platoon," Patrick worked the day shift from nine a.m. to six p.m. half the week and then rotated to the night shift from six p.m. to nine a.m. for the other half, averaging twelve hours of work a day or seventy-two hours a week. He had a twenty-four-hour leave period once a week. Now he was able to sleep at home more often, although the battalion chief always remained on call.

With the new schedule, Patrick no longer walked home for meals. Whenever son Paul was available, his mother sent him to Fulton Street with a hot lunch or supper. Mary Ann kept her home-made soup steaming hot in a sealed jar and she tightly covered the dish of meat, potatoes and vegetables. Paul took a subway or the trolley over the Brooklyn Bridge and walked west to fire headquarters. One particular fireman there would tease him by blocking his way up the stairs to the chief's office, threatening to steal the dinner. Paul soon got tired of the teasing and had to squelch his desire to yell up to his father to call off the joker.

The youngster usually sat and chatted while Patrick ate, and often the father accompanied his son down to the street to buy apples or oranges for Paul to carry home. The local street vendors all knew Patrick. "No, don't buy these today, Chief," they'd say, "they're not too good. Buy those others."

When no lunch could be brought from home, Patrick sometimes sent out his order with a young fire buff who worked in the area and who lingered about the firehouse during his lunch hour. Patrick's favorite was the beef-and-bean sandwich that cost fifteen cents at Hitchcock's on Park Row. The Chief sought to "burn off" his sizable lunches on daily walks across the Brooklyn Bridge and on the handball court on the roof of 193 Fulton. Though in his early fifties, Patrick was still a serious contender at handball.

Vigorous walking remained a favorite physical activity. One day after working the night shift, coming home and having breakfast, Patrick challenged Paul with "I'll walk you to Coney Island," and off they went on the twelve-mile hike. Paul felt lucky that his father was willing to trolley home.

Some Sunday afternoons Patrick and Paul took a train to Coney Island, walked the whole length of the beach and then continued on to Sheepshead Bay to watch the commercial fishing boats returning with their catch. Patrick always asked which fish were running.

These casual observations along Sheepshead Bay lured Patrick into casting a line himself. Paul was his only companion in the pursuit of deep-sea fishing, Joe having reneged after a bout of sea-sickness on his first trip out. The father, arriving home from the night shift, greeted Paul with, "Get the fishing gear ready!" Down into the subway they would go with their awkward rods and tackle, arriving at Sheepshead Bay to catch the ten a.m. boat. One wintry day they brought home so much codfish that preserving it became the problem. Paul fetched a discarded butter tub from behind the neighborhood grocery store and father and son filled it by alternating a layer of salt and a layer of fish. The tub was positioned outside the kitchen door and twice a week Mary Ann dipped in for a cod, washed off the salt and tried to invent a new way of serving it.

Sometimes Patrick and Paul rented a small rowboat and drifted around the coastal waters fringing the Bay. Throwing clam shells overboard to lure the cod, they dropped their primitive hand lines using clam chunks for bait. Paul remembered his feeling of both triumph and despair when two fish, weighing some fifteen pounds each, attached themselves to his hook. His cry for help was in vain. "*You* got them on there, *you* pull them out." But Patrick's fear of losing several potential dinners or of seeing the rowboat capsize beneath them finally moved him to lend the strength of his arm to the struggling Paul.

First Battalion Headquarters on Fulton Street was just west of old St. Paul's church with its large enclosed graveyard and tombstones dating from the seventeen hundreds. This solitary block is still an oasis amid the press of circling traffic and tall commercial buildings bordering it on all sides. Most people employed in the area moved by without seeing St. Paul's. But Patrick felt its constant presence and it reminded him of a plane of existence as real to him as the fires he fought and the battalion he supervised. It inspired another of his poems, "When Bells Call Men to Prayer," most likely scratched out at his desk in the office on the second floor of 193 Fulton.

> Upon Broadway I stood one day
> The midday hour was nigh.
> To watch those seething crowds that sway
> When rushing madly by.
> There ringing church bells I did hear
> From steeple high in air,
> The Angelus distinct and clear
> Was calling me to prayer.
>
> But what is prayer to busy men,
> Lost time and nothing more,
> Rank superstition and nonsense,
> To busy men a bore.
> Their time is money, so they say,
> Whom none but fools could spare,
> Then why should they attention pay
> When bells call them to prayer.
>
> Just then my eyes through churchyard bars
> Fell on the other side,
> Where many years, sun, moon and stars
> Saw just such men abide,
> Who in the ages long past by
> Were filled with earthly care
> And had not time to doff a hat
> When bells called them to prayer.
>
> But listen now to what they say,

Tis written there on stone,
To all of you who pass this way
We, too, were flesh and bone.
We now are clay, so will you be
Then why of clay such care?
Remember man, Eternity,
When bells call you to prayer

Wall Street, the heart of New York's financial district, lies just six blocks south of Fulton and was within Patrick's territory as 1st Battalion chief. He was the fire official who arrived at Wall Street shortly after noon on September 16, 1920. A car loaded with explosives had blown up outside the windows of J.P. Morgan & Co. during the lunch hour when hundreds of company officers, brokers and employees were on the streets. The crime was never solved, but popular suspicion had it that the deed was perpetrated by some disappointed dabbler in stocks.

In an interview Patrick gave years later to a staff writer of the New York *World Telegram*, he called the Wall Street explosion the most terrifying episode of his career.

I was in the truck just fixing to have a cup of tea when the explosion went off. I recalled they were ripping down a building on Broadway and I thought something might have gone wrong there. I turned to my chauffeur and said, "If that's an explosion, and I think it is, you'd better get ready to call out all the ambulances in the city." All of lower Manhattan had shivered.

A moment after I spoke the bell came in from Pine and Nassau. By the time I got there, every able-bodied person had fled for their lives fearing more bombs would go off any minute. I saw men with heads blown off, or legs, or arms. Glass was strewn up and down Wall Street like hailstones. Ours was a frightful job. There were two hundred injured persons to see after and about forty dead to take away. The damage to property was over a million dollars. It was a long time before I got my cup of tea that day.[1]

CHAPTER SEVEN

Father and Sons

1920 - 1927

Michael Walsh resigned his commission in the Navy soon after Armistice Day and took up the law practice he had already begun as a law student with the firm of Louis Charles Wills at 26 Court Street near Borough Hall in Brooklyn. He had plans to begin a new life on another level as well since he was engaged to be married to Catherine Dundon, the young woman he had known since grade school. Catherine recalled years later that, once engaged to Michael, she felt at liberty to telephone him at home when the need arose. If the father happened to answer the phone, however, his brusque firehouse manner would intimidate her and she would hang up without identifying herself.

Michael and Catherine were married in November, 1919. They were fortunate that Jerry, their best man, was present for the wedding because he arrived from Europe aboard the *George Washington* just two days before. Since Jack, the seminarian in Washington, could not come home, Michael and Catherine spent their honeymoon visiting him. The only snapshots that remain are those of the couple standing together with the white-robed Jack, his religious house in the background.

Michael felt close to his brother Jack and missed his presence at the wedding. But the couple's honeymoon in Washington probably said something more about the Walshes. In Michael's thinking, as of course in Patrick's, marriage was a noble and holy vocation and it seemed suitable, when entering it, to embark on a type of pilgrimage that the trip to the seminary represented. Such a trip was Michael's prayer for blessings on their married life. Catherine accepted Michael's initiative, but it was hardly her idea of a honeymoon. She also wanted all the blessings of a Catholic wedding but would have preferred the traditional wedding trip, far from the companionship of other Walshes. The couple came home from Washington to Brooklyn and settled into an apartment on Madison Street, in the Bedford-Stuyvesant section.

Three years later Jerry Walsh married Betty Resker. They had met shortly after Jerry was discharged from the service at the end of 1919. Betty remembered him as the most heavy-set of the boys, with a round face whose ready smile was often hidden behind his dead-pan humor. He was a volunteer usher during Sunday Mass at St. Charles and, if Betty happened to be at the same Mass, he would give her special recognition by holding the collection basket under her nose until he thought her donation large enough.

Michael had set the tradition and Jerry followed. He and Betty took off on their honeymoon to visit Jack in Washington, a gesture Jerry knew would please his parents. The couple took a few day trips out of the capital and one snapshot shows Jerry and Betty seated on a bench with George Washington's Mount Vernon home in the background. Jerry, in three-piece shirt, stiff collar and tie, has his arm around Betty and sits casually, legs apart, one knee in her direction. He looks tall and broad, though not stout, has a round, handsome, smiling face, and his eyes are half-closed against the September sunshine.

Betty Walsh was drawn into the family orbit as Catherine had been. Saturday night meant dinner at 155 State Street because "Pop" was happiest when his family surrounded him. Joseph was a law student and also bringing a steady girl friend to the Saturday gatherings. The after-dinner card games continued and Mary Ann packaged leftover food for each couple to take home.

Patrick presided at these gatherings with loud conversation and laughter. Even as he had enjoyed spending free time with his growing children, so much more did he savor the interplay with them as adults. Through his children, Patrick extended himself into a larger world. They embodied his values and aspirations and their accomplishments were at least as precious as his own.

It is hard to determine if one son or another wanted to break away from the tightly knit circle. None took the step. Michael, and later Joseph, fully engaged in their own careers and marriages, were always attuned to Pop and his needs, and were always ready to consult Pop on matters large and small.

Jerry seldom missed a family gathering and rivaled Pop as the liveliest of the group. His sense of humor provided entertainment when the card game got dull and often eased tensions when Patrick argued too aggressively. But if anyone wanted, from time to time, to breathe some air outside the family enclave, it was most likely Jerry. Although his happy personality could deflect tension, it could not eliminate it. And Jerry himself was often the target of Patrick's criticisms. Until Jerry settled on a steady line of work, with some promise of a future, Patrick would never let matters rest between them.

Patrick's power over his children was the strongest kind. They internalized his values — reverence for authority, devotion to the Catholic religion and to a spirit of service, pursuit of a worthy career and achievement within it. Since these values became their own, they measured their success or failure just as he would. Since they regarded their father as the epitome of these values, they could not have shed his influence easily had they even tried.

Walsh togetherness was not just reserved for Saturday meals and cards. Father and sons met whenever they could to play handball. Patrick did a lot of shouting on the court, chastising a partner for a lame shot, goading on his opponents or, occasionally, praising a well-won point.

Michael, whose law office was close to Brooklyn Heights, often walked to State Street to have lunch with his mother. His mother-in-law shared the Flatbush apartment that he and Catherine had moved to and it was Mamie Dundon who cooked the evening meal. Between mother and mother-in-law, Michael put on weight.

In November, 1923, Michael and Catherine's first child was born — a son, Francis. Patrick was delighted at the arrival of a grandchild

Patrick as Battalion Chief,
circa 1922

and the start of a new Walsh generation.

Once or twice a year between 1919 and 1924, with or without their children, Patrick and Mary Ann traveled to Washington to visit Jack at his seminary. They liked taking advantage of a special weekend B & O excursion train between New York and the capital. It left Penn Station at midnight on Saturday, arriving in Washington at six a.m. Sunday. The return train departed Washington at six p.m. the same Sunday, reaching New York at midnight. Paul remembered the return trip on hot summer nights, with dirt and soot from the coal-fueled locomotives flying through the open windows. He also remembered trying to keep awake in class those Monday mornings.

Jack was ordained to the priesthood in Washington in June, 1924. Patrick reserved an entire car on the railroad to carry as many relatives and friends as possible to attend this solemn occasion. The father later expressed his feelings of awe and gratitude in a poem he entitled simply "Ordination of a Son — June 1924."

> We thank the Lord we see today
> Our absent son, so long away
> We thank the Lord that he did find
> The path the Master hath outlined.
>
> Through thorns and briers he saw revealed
> A shining gem to us concealed
> Most priceless treasure worth all strife
> A priest of God, a holy life.
>
> When came the call from Gallilee,
> "Take up your cross and follow Me,"
> The very demons out of hell
> Required from him eternal care,
> Should he avoid their tempters' snare.
>
> The silent cloister that he sought
> Intensified their mighty wrath.
> Weep, Satan, weep, while we rejoice
> Today we see the Master's choice
> Upon God's altar, where he stands,

The Sacred Host within his hands.
Oh! may he never cease that strife
'Til he attain that perfect life
Which Dominic, that saint sublime,
Marked out for him in ancient time.

The image of battle surfaces again, the struggle between God
and the Devil, good and evil — in prior poems, it had been my
country and the invader. Life was warfare and the stakes were clear
since good and evil were readily discernible. A choice for the good,
and a lifelong commitment to it, were sure to involve continuous
battle. Man's will, informed by the grace of God, could achieve
victory in the end.

Patrick had taken the examination for Deputy Chief several
years before he received an appointment. When the legal life of the
civil service list expired in 1923, only three appointments had been
made and Patrick's name had moved up to second place. He had to
retake the examination and hope for a high enough position on the
new list to succeed in the next round of appointments. His promotion finally came in May of 1925, when he was named Deputy Chief
of the 11th Division, supervising several battalions in the Greenpoint,
Brooklyn, area. This section of the city was new to him and he had
to work quickly to familiarize himself with the terrain. As deputy
chief he would be expected to have detailed knowledge of the fire
hazards of his district, the street patterns, major buildings, entrances,
exits, and so on.

The new assignment lasted only a year and a half. In November, 1926, he was chosen to fill one of only three assistant chief
positions in the department. He was now referred to as "Patrick
Walsh No. 1" to distinguish him from several other Patrick Walshes in
the fireman ranks. Although it was an enviable promotion and a
boost to his career ambitions, Patrick entertained mixed feelings
about it. As assistant chief he would have to move out of the
firehouse and into the department's administrative offices on the

eleventh floor of the Municipal Building on Chambers Street, in charge now of the Bureau of Fire Prevention.

Fire prevention has nothing of the glamour of fire fighting. Fighting a fire is a highly visible enterprise, exciting and often heroic. The result of preventing fires is seldom noticed. Who is to say how many lives were saved and how much property was preserved because measures had been taken to prevent a fire from happening in the first place? Fire prevention does not lend itself to headline stories, and yet the most important service is being performed there.

The notion that fire prevention should be undertaken in any organized sense only surfaced when the Triangle Shirtwaist Factory was in ashes and one hundred forty-seven lives, most of them young women, had been lost. New York City's Bureau of Fire Prevention was a pioneer in the field among state and city bureaucracies. Its early activities, in 1911 and beyond, brought about improvements in the construction and outfitting of buildings: stair enclosures, fire escapes, sprinklers, interior fire alarms, watchman services, among others. New York City's bureau was the first to recognize the value of having an emergency maintenance man in the average big building and, by 1929, this had become a requirement by law.

The addition of these features was expensive, however, and New York businesses chafed at their new obligations. From time to time business interests were influential in the drafting of legislation aimed at curbing or even destroying the Bureau of Fire Prevention. Unsuccessful in this effort, opponents were able, in 1932, to remove the function from the fire department and from Patrick's supervision and assign it to the city's Department of Buildings. There the enforcement of fire prevention was not given high priority and the department maneuvered behind the scenes until it was able to reclaim the bureau in 1938.[1]

It did not take long, however, before Patrick brought his usual enthusiasm to the new assignment. He set about reorganizing the bureau, improving systems for inspections, accounting and record-keeping. He found ways to expedite the bureau's response to blueprints and other documents that private builders were required to submit for approval. His efforts at raising the general efficiency of the bureau earned for him the department's Administration Medal for 1927, awarded only on occasion for some outstanding administrative innovation. In a year's time Patrick proved to himself and to his superiors that he could manage an administrative job successfully.

Although largely confined as assistant chief to an office in the Municipal Building, Patrick did not allow administration to totally replace fire fighting. He was still expected to attend serious fires and he interpreted the term liberally. While dedicating himself to the very necessary duties of fire prevention, he was as captivated by fire fighting in the 1920's and 1930's as he had been at the start of his career.

By the fall of 1924, Patrick and Mary Ann had given up the house at 155 State Street and moved into a seven-room apartment some eight blocks away, at 80 Montague Street, corner of Hicks. Mary Ann was in her early sixties and had begun to find housekeeping in a four-story home too tiring. The new Montague Street apartment was ample, with bedroom space for the couple as well as for Joe, Mary and Paul who still lived at home. The dining room was large and the Saturday night gatherings of the clan would continue unrestricted.

In contrast to the quiet of their neighborhood on State Street, Montague was the commercial corridor of Brooklyn Heights. Their new apartment occupied the third of a four-story building, above a drug store and across Hicks Street from the Bossert, one of Brooklyn's few prominent hotels. Davidson and Buckley Apothecary Shop employed four pharmacists and included a large soda fountain in its ground-floor store. Mr. Buckley, whose bushy white beard and peculiar brimmed hat gave him the look of a Southern colonel, was always on the scene commanding operations. Patrick introduced himself as the upstairs neighbor and, when the manager of the soda fountain quit his job, Patrick was the first to hear about it.

Jerry was twenty-seven and two years married. He was dissatisfied with the office job he held in a small Brooklyn industry. With Patrick as intermediary he now was hired by Mr. Buckley to manage the luncheonette/soda fountain with its busy corner store trade. Joseph, twenty-two and a law school student, helped his brother part time, both at the counter and in the bookkeeping. The two had some experience from jobs they had worked in a luncheonette located under the Hotel St. George, but neither had ever tried management. Paul, a freshman at Fordham College, served as third man when needed. He especially liked preparing the syrups which he boiled for hours. Sundaes were topped with fresh strawberries or pineapple and a rivalry grew among the brothers as to who could concoct the most original sundae and the most extravagant name. Their efforts brought a brisk business from the Brooklyn Heights Seminary girls who arrived in numbers when school was dismissed each afternoon.

Paul, decades later, recalled the fun of the enterprise but, to Jerry and Joe, the running of a luncheonette was serious hard work for which neither was adequately prepared. Despite their planning and the energy they expended or the consultations with their father and Mr. Buckley, their business experiment lasted only a year. Patrick was upset the boys could not make a go of the operation and was not slow in communicating his feelings to them.

Joe could continue his law studies and launch a career of his own. For Jerry this was a stressful time. He alone of the five sons had not gone to college nor pursued a consistent line of work. At age twenty-eight he still felt answerable to his father. Jerry now threw himself into searching for another job, one that would at least be steady, that would prove his seriousness. He applied and was accepted for a clerk's position with the Interborough Rapid Transit System, better known as the IRT subway line.

Joe had introduced Mary Bergen to the family in 1922 and had brought her home regularly ever since. Mary Ann knew that sensible Joseph was concentrating on his law practice and would get around to other segments of his life in due time. Whether the mother tactfully prompted Joe or Mary Bergen nudged him, or Joe deliberated on his own that the right time had come, Joe and Mary were married in May of 1927. Wife Mary was always known in the family as Mary Bergen to avoid confusing her with Mary, daughter and sister.

Father Jack celebrated the nuptial mass and performed the marriage ceremony. It was the occasion for a formal family photograph, the last taken of all the members together. Patrick was fifty-eight now and the receding hairline above his ruddy, oval face made him look older. Mary Ann was a solid, stocky figure in a long, loose-fitting organdy coat, chest opened to a bodice insert with pearls around her bare neck. Her square, bespectacled face beneath a high bun hairdo wore an expression of calm and peace. The five brothers dressed in black, four in formal cutaway suits with white winged collars and one in the black suit and Roman collar of his priesthood. Michael, at thirty-three, had the stocky build of his parents, with full oval face, round nose and dark complexion. Father Jack, thirty-one, had a bespectacled, scholarly demeanor, with stiff wavy hair brushed back from a high forehead. Jerry, thirty, and almost six feet, was the tallest of the brothers and the most heavy-set, with a round, stout face and high cheek bones. Joseph, the twenty-four year old groom, was the blondest of the group, with wavy hair and intense blue eyes. Paul, twenty, had the slightest build, an aquiline nose, the handsomest of the brothers. Mary Bergen was the smiling bride in white satin and Catherine and Betty completed the group, the daughters-in-law having developed a certain kinship in their shared status at the periphery of the clan. Francis, the only grandchild, was also included in the celebration, a round, blond, full-faced three-year-old in his belted, one-piece white suit, white knee socks and black patent-leather pumps. It was the last time Patrick's children were all gathered in one place before the younger ones set out on their own chosen paths.

Paul finished his third year at Fordham College the next month and followed his brother Jack into the Dominican Order. He took the train to Kentucky where the novitiate was located at St. Rose Priory in Springfield. Now there were two sons lawyers and two sons priests—or, as Patrick would repeatedly quip, "Two to keep me out of jail and two to keep me out of hell."

A third event in 1927 was as emotional for Patrick as the wedding of one son or another's departure for the seminary. He visited Ireland for the first time since he had sailed away almost forty years

Joseph Walsh and Mary Bergen wed, 1927. STANDING LEFT TO RIGHT:
Jerry, Paul, Betty, Father Jack, Kitty, Michael, Mary;
SEATED: Patrick, Mary Bergen, Joseph, Mary Ann, Francis.

before. This was a real vacation, one he had never taken since joining the fire department. Patrick, Mary Ann and daughter Mary Florence set sail from New York in September, en route for Cobh, the harbor "city of tears" through which waves of Irish had departed their country and only a trickle returned.

Patrick had maintained an interest over the years in the Irish uprisings, conflicts and debates that propelled the movement toward independence from England. Paul remembered occasions when he accompanied his father to Irish-American rallies in New York City. Patrick admired Eamon de Valera, a spokesman for the unification of northern and southern Ireland, who became the Republic's first president.

For Patrick and Mary Ann, returning to Ireland was like entering a time warp. Ballydine in County Tipperary was still the same three farms. Not only had Patrick and Mary Ann's birthplaces remained in their families, but the farm in between, owned by the Murphy's in Patrick's youth, had been bought by Mary Ann's sister Johanna with her husband Owen Davern. Ballydine was a clan enclave.

The front of the Walsh home was still a pub and general store managed by Patrick's youngest sister, Alice. Mary Ann's brother Tom raised a dairy herd on her family's lands. One would have to look closely to see any changes — the plow and reaper in the sheds were more refined than the 1888 models. But the exterior of the buildings and the surrounding fields had persisted in timeless fashion. Patrick stood on the rise of land in front of his old house and gazed on the same scene that had so impressed him in his boyhood—the Galty Mountains to the south, the more distant Knockmealdown Mountains to the east, the Rock of Cashel guarding the other end of the valley and the Suir River cutting its way across the ripe fields.

Patrick's sister Alice was the only family member left in Ireland, since Bridget and Anna had long since emigrated to the States and Jack had died in Belgium. Mary Ann, however, had eight of her brothers and sisters to get to know again after decades of separation. The partition of Ireland into the Republic of the south and the six counties still linked to Britain in the north had been a major source of contention since the civil war of 1922-1923, and had left some of the Ryans divided and embittered. Two of Mary Ann's brothers had not talked to their sons since that war. But Mary Ann enjoyed one especially happy reunion at the Trappist abbey in Roscrea where John Ryan, closest to Mary Ann in age, had been a cloistered brother for over thirty years.

Patrick compared himself to that New Yorker who lives his whole life within view of the Statue of Liberty yet never visits it. The Rock of Cashel was one of Ireland's revered sites, drawing pilgrim and tourist alike. It had been part of Patrick's childhood scene, rising up as an impregnable fortress on the other side of the valley. But he had left the country at nineteen without ever having gone there. Now, with keen interest, he climbed the cobblestone road at the edge of the town of Cashel leading up the steep hill to a plateau of rock and the ancient ruins of cathedral, castle and tower. Patrick found the site "hoary with antiquity." First to place armaments upon this natural fortification in the year 370 was Corc, the legendary King of Munster. About the year 450 St. Patrick himself is credited with establishing the seat of a church diocese on the Rock and anointing an archbishop there. Although other churches must have preceded it on the site, the oldest surviving limestone structure is Cormac's Chapel, consecrated in 1134 by Cormac McCarthy, King and Bishop. It is a remarkable building with Romanesque features, an influence believed to have entered Ireland through the missionary work of Irish monks in Twelfth Century Germany.

This chapel, together with the skeleton of cathedral and castle which make up the fortress-like monument, are flanked at their base by stretches of tombstones sitting up like dwarfs on the grassy slopes. Families with local roots from the seventeenth and eighteenth centuries had been permitted to bury their dead on the holy grounds of the Rock. Patrick found the Walsh graves clustered together at the side of Cormac's Chapel, the names of his parents and grandparents clearly readable on the stones. He knelt on the earth at the grave of his great-grandfather, John Walsh , born in 1760. From this elevated spot, Patrick surveyed the fertile valleys in all directions, the "Golden

Vale" of Tipperary, the land of his fathers which he had left behind but which had never completely loosened its grip on him.

CHAPTER EIGHT

Clan Togetherness

1928 - 1934

 For Mary Florence the trip to Ireland was a farewell gift from her parents. Mary had told them some months before that she had made up her mind to become a nun and enter the Order of the Religious of the Cenacle.

Mary Florence, the special child, the only girl who survived, absorbed her parents' values as her brothers had. While enrolled in normal school, or teacher's training, she and friends from St. Charles parish began taking the subway to the Upper West Side for periodic weekends of retreat at the Cenacle Convent on Riverside Drive. When Mary felt the attraction of a religious vocation, the life of these Cenacle nuns began to interest her.

Mary was waiting for the right moment to tell Patrick about her decision and it soon came. She had taken the New York State licensing examination after completing teacher's training. When the envelope arrived with the news that she had not received a passing grade, she decided to say nothing about it since she would not be needing the license anyway. Instead she told her father of her desire to enter religious life. She had planned to announce this decision anyway and it was especially pleasant to avoid mention of failing grades.

In February, 1928, a few months after her twenty-third birthday, Mary left home for a life in the convent. Michael drove Mary, Patrick and Mary Ann the fifty miles to Lake Ronkonkoma on Long Island where the Order's novitiate was located on four hundred acres of farmland and forest. This Cenacle property was the former estate of Maude Adams, perhaps the most celebrated American actress of the early years of the century, who had brought Peter Pan to life on the Broadway stage in more than fifteen hundred performances. Maude Adams was befriended over the years by the Cenacle nuns at their convent on Riverside Drive in Manhattan. She liked to escape there for rest and quiet between performances during her active stage career. In 1927 she showed her appreciation by making the gift of the Lake Ronkonkoma land and houses to the Order.

The Religious of the Cenacle pursued a semicloistered life. Although the family would be allowed to visit, Mary herself could never leave the convent grounds. But compared to Paul who trained in Kentucky, Illinois and Ohio, Mary Florence, on Long Island, was in her parents' backyard. The Cenacle's rules for novices limited family visits to one Sunday afternoon in three months. Most likely the Cenacle nuns did not anticipate Chief Walsh's definition of a family visit. Everybody came: Michael and Catherine with young Frank, the new baby Jack, and Catherine's mother; Jerry and Betty, Joseph and Mary Bergen. On pleasant days they sat out on benches in some corner of the wooded grounds, clustered around the young nun in purple and black robes and white veil. Even Mary's face was only partially visible behind the stiff white oval fluting. When weather was cold or rainy, the family occupied one of the house's large parlors. Late afternoon Benediction in the chapel, where the chanting nuns could be glimpsed for the last time behind the choir gate, was the cue for relatives to depart.

In the late 1920's, Joseph and Mary began to look for a summer vacation spot to escape the humid heat of New York City. At the suggestion of friends they wrote to Faulkner's Lodge on Blue Mountain Lake in the Adirondack Mountains of New York State. Joe had only two weeks' vacation from Sinclair Oil Company's legal department and a tolerable drive to the Adirondacks took almost two days. But Joe and Mary found the natural beauty and isolation of the spot immensely appealing and they began a series of summer visits that continued for thirty-five years. Joe was relaxed and happy when he could fish and play golf, and Mary spent that time with other ladies in the wicker rocking chairs on the front porch of the lodge.

In summer, 1930, Patrick and Mary Ann accepted Joe's invitation and took the train to Glens Falls where Joe met them and drove them the seventy-five miles north to Blue Mountain Lake. It was the first of many such trips for Patrick. During the 1930 visit, he tried his hand at golf. Mike and Joe had both been urging him to try the game since, by age sixty, his favorite handball was too physically exhausting.

Patrick never became a competitive golfer but he enjoyed what were to become regular outings with Joe at courses in Queens and on Long Island. Mike joined them as often as he could. With careless impatience, Patrick hacked his way around a course. Playing the game left-handed, he would approach the ball, swing mightily without pause or calculation, and "damn" the scorekeeper who put him down for one hundred and twenty strokes!

His energy did not let up, though the pace of the game was slower than handball or football. On one occasion when he was already in his seventies he played eighteen holes with Joe in the morning, went into the clubhouse for a light lunch, and returned to play eighteen holes in the afternoon.

As children matured and needed their mother's attention less and as the housing quarters they occupied got smaller, Mary Ann devoted more of her time to events in St. Charles parish. Each day began at Mass with Patrick and she often returned to the church in the afternoon to join other women in planning some fund-raising event or to wash and iron altar linens or perform any other needed task. Some afternoons she made hospital visits to sick members of the parish. But when the last of the children left home, she keenly felt their absence.

In the fall of 1928, about six months after Mary had gone, Paul was transferred to the Dominican House of Studies in River Forest, Illinois, and urged his parents to come for a visit the following spring. Patrick, the immigrant patriot who esteemed his country so highly, had never journeyed west of New Jersey in the forty years he lived in America. The itinerary for this new trip was exciting. Joseph had volunteered to drive them to River Forest, a suburb of Chicago. After a week's visit with Paul, the couple would return by boarding a boat on Lake Michigan at the port of Chicago and travel through the Great Lakes to Buffalo, going the entire length of Lake Michigan, Lake Huron and Lake Erie. From Buffalo they would take a train ride home across New York State. For Patrick this was the opportunity to see firsthand the immensity of the country, the endless stretches of farmland in Pennsylvania, Indiana, Illinois. How different it was from the Irish farm country of his boyhood. How long since he had worked a plow and, strangely, how little he had missed it. The return trip through the Great Lakes was as impressive as the trip out, the grandeur of these inland waterways which seemed small oceans to the boat plowing across them.

The visit to River Forest in spring of 1929 began a long friendship between the assistant fire chief and his wife and the twenty-five seminarians in Paul's class. After his brother Jerry, Paul was by nature the most outgoing of the family, with a ready wit and quick grasp of the humorous side of a situation. His infectious laughter rose above the noise level of any group he was with. His popularity with his classmates made it easy for them to adopt his parents. Behind Patrick's sometimes crusty demeanor, the students saw the source of his son's sense of humor. Patrick told anecdotes in loud, rapid-fire delivery, climaxed by an eruption of laughter that swept along his listeners in its tide. For Mary Ann, it was easier to think that she had adopted the twenty-five young men than that she had give up her youngest child. Soon the mother began mailing them regular boxes of treats. When a giant carton of candy bars arrived one Halloween, the students figured, "Ole man Walsh had a fire in a candy factory." At ordination six years later, when Patrick and Mary Ann gave to each of the twenty who had persevered to the priesthood a set of vestments for Mass, the conclusion was, "Ole man Walsh had a fire in a bank."

At the end of a three-year course of studies in River Forest, Paul and his class were transferred in 1931 to the Dominican Priory in Somerset, Ohio, where Jack had spent his first year away from home. Father Jack, stationed at that time in Jersey City, was assigned to preach a church mission in the Midwest and afterward took a side trip to visit Paul in Somerset. Jack's visit happened to coincide with a high-level session of the Dominican Provincial Council to determine the election of a new prior for the house. The outcome of the election caucus that week was the surprise drafting of the visitor, Jack. He thus became prior of St. Joseph's, presiding over a community in which his brother was a student.

With two sons living in the same house, little could keep Patrick and Mary Ann from making the trip to see them that summer. And the clan traveled with them. Joe and Mary drove their parents in one car, followed by Mike and Catherine with young Frank and Jack in a second. Catherine's mother had stayed home with the year-old baby Mary Florence.

A series of snapshots survive that Ohio reunion of summer 1931. One shows three rows of twenty-two smiling, white-robed Dominicans, the sameness of the subjects' appearance broken only by the presence of the two youngsters — seven-year-old Frank standing in their midst and Prior Jack Walsh clasping in his lap his three-year-old namesake nephew. The other snapshots give the impression the Walsh family visit that summer became holiday time at the seminary. One afternoon Patrick arranged a truck and convoy of cars to carry the whole class for swimming and a picnic at Buckeye Lake, some thirty miles away on the road to Columbus. Solid and paunchy at sixty-two, Patrick slid into the role of summer camp program director, moving about in his quick-motion manner with shirtsleeves rolled to the elbows and tie correctly in place, his face round and clean-shaven, hairline barely visible halfway back on his scalp. As much as Patrick seemed constantly in motion, Mary Ann was still, whether she was sitting in a lawn chair or walking about in her even, gliding step. She was always formally dressed in dark colors and was seldom seen without her high straw hat. The somber tone of her outfits was most apparent when her daughters-in-law were with her in their white or pastel summer dresses and permanent-waved hair in the 1930 fashion.

Prior Jack took some time off for a golf outing wearing his plus

Patrick golfing with his sons.
LEFT TO RIGHT: *Prior Jack, Joseph, Mike,*
Patrick, a Dominican priest holding young Jack.

The seminarians cool off. LOWER LEFT ON THE TRIANGLE:
Mike, Frank and Joe. Jack at edge of pool, with Patrick behind.

Somerset, Ohio, 1931. Young Frank and Jack with class of Dominican seminarians.

fours as did Patrick, Mike and Joe. Patrick's spirits soared at spending a day on the golf course with three sons. The whole vacation in Somerset was his idea of perfect rest and enjoyment.

When Paul's year of study in Ohio ended, he left Somerset and his brother Jack. The prior stayed on and Paul returned with his classmates to the East Coast for the final three years of training at the Dominican House of Studies in Washington where Jack had also spent his seminary years. The Washington Dominicans owned a beach house in Ocean City, Maryland, and over the following three summers, the Walshes dropped in on them.

Mary Ann never forgot her first visit to Ocean City in 1932. A hurricane struck the coast with winds that took a hundred feet of the boardwalk and placed it on an adjoining side street. Sand was driven about so fiercely that it scratched the paint off the automobiles parked by the beach. The storm haunted her dreams for months.

The experience of a hurricane did not deter the Walshes from returning to Ocean City in the summer of 1933. Michael took his camera and snapped pictures everywhere. Frank, age nine, Jack, five, and Mary Florence, three, all went to Ocean City to visit their Dominican uncle. Baby Kathleen stayed home with Grandma Dundon.

The best snapshot is of the men in their one-piece black swimsuits, just emerged from the waves, the surf pounding behind them and the young children clinging to their arms. For Patrick, swimming was an exercise to be performed vigorously. He liked to spend a half hour following a set course back and forth beyond the breakers. Coming out of the water, he went directly to his room to put on clothes. Lying about on the beach was not to his liking.

One afternoon Patrick rented a small excursion boat for an hour's cruise along the shoreline. Fourteen set out, Patrick and Mary Ann, Michael and Catherine, Joe and Mary, the three youngsters, Paul and four of his classmates. One of these classmates was Brother Quentin whose quick-wits and humor made him a favorite. A strong sea breeze whipped off Brother Quentin's hat and carried it into the water. Luckily, a German Shepherd dog, upon command of its owner, dove in to retrieve the soggy hat. Brother Quentin and his hat became a favorite, often repeated story.

On most days three wooden beach chairs were set up on the sand in the makeshift shade of twin beach umbrellas. One was for Mary Ann who relaxed in the canvass seat, feet on the foot rest, looking much as she might in Brooklyn, or anywhere else, in her full-length dress, shoes and stockings. Catherine and Mary Bergen, in more casual dresses, occupied the other beach chairs. The three women sat close enough to the water's edge to watch the men cavort and ensure that someone kept an eye on the children. Often a few seminarians would be stretched out on the sand by the chairs, heckling the swimmers and entertaining the women with jokes and stories.

In all the pictures taken, first in Ohio and later at Ocean City, Jerry and Betty are noticeably absent. Perhaps it was easier for the lawyers than for the office worker to arrange his time off from work. On the other hand, perhaps there was reluctance in Jerry to spend his brief two weeks' vacation on family trips to religious houses. In this tight-knit family, his absence must have been felt by all.

One snapshot survives from 1934, the last summer at Ocean City. It was taken on the sidewalk outside the tourist home where the family stayed and it looks like the moment of departure. The figure in the group who had changed most in the year's time was Mary Ann. Gone was her native portliness, her dress hanging a bit limply on her thinner frame. At seventy-one, her face had become drawn and heavily lined. Whether for this reason or some other, the expression on the round, stout face of Patrick registered deep concern.

Paul and his classmates had been ordained in Washington in June of 1934 and Patrick had once again led a caravan of family and friends to witness a second son receive the sacrament of Holy Orders. The celebration which followed was especially warm since Paul's class by then regarded the Walshes as family.

A week following ordination, Paul said his first Mass in the chapel of the Cenacle on Riverside Drive in Manhattan where Mary was temporarily stationed. The Great White Fleet of the U.S. Navy,

Ocean City, Maryland, 1933.
Emerging from the surf, LEFT TO RIGHT:
Michael holding Mary Florence, Paul, Jack, Frank, Joe, Patrick.

Leaving Ocean City, 1934.

which included some fourteen battleships, was docked in New York harbor at that time. At the most sacred moment of the Mass, the Consecration, all guns on board suddenly sounded an unknowing salute.

CHAPTER NINE

Plunging into Fires

1932 - 1935

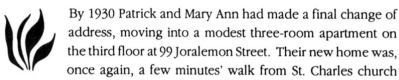 By 1930 Patrick and Mary Ann had made a final change of address, moving into a modest three-room apartment on the third floor at 99 Joralemon Street. Their new home was, once again, a few minutes' walk from St. Charles church which had been for them over the years, both physically and symbolically, the hub of their everyday lives. Though the new apartment was smaller, the Saturday night dinner for the family and the games of Setback resumed their familiar rhythms.

The Assistant Chief of Department spent the required hours at his desk in the Municipal Building. But at the earliest indication that it might be his duty to appear at the scene of a fire, he was into his uniform and on his way. One fire that he long remembered occurred at a favorite haunt of his, Coney Island.

Brooklyn might have been the "city of churches" to some people; to many more it was Coney Island. In its vintage days (1897-1940), Coney Island was queen of amusement parks. One author recounts that, before 1905, the area was a weekend writers' colony, a fashionable resort and a hangout for New York mobsters at the same time. The famous amusement park section emerged only gradually. After trolleys and trains linked Coney Island to the rest of the city, a vast cross-section of people gained access to its beaches, its rides and its hoopla. By 1920 Coney Island had become a mecca for millions of city dwellers.[1]

The rolling surf and the brisk salt air at Coney Island always attracted Patrick. He had loved to walk the beach with the children tagging after him, promising them a ride on the merry-go-round if they quickened their pace. (The famous boardwalk only opened in 1923.) With Paul, a high school student in the early 1920's, he had taken long hikes — either walking the whole distance from Brooklyn Heights to the beach or going by train and walking the length of Coney Island, Brighton Beach, Sheepshead Bay and Manhattan Beach.

On July 13, 1932, Patrick rode to Coney Island in his red chief's car. It had been a hot day that drew some 200,000 people to the shore. The origin of the fire was never made clear, but when Patrick arrived on the scene at the sounding of the fifth alarm, four solid blocks were aflame, including seven of the largest bathhouses and a thousand feet of boardwalk. Five thousand persons were made homeless and more than a hundred autos destroyed.

At the first shouts of "Fire!" crowds of bathers had rushed to the bathhouse offices, clamoring for the wallets and valuables they had checked. Entry to these bathhouses was soon sealed off and one sixty-year-old beach bum stood behind the cordon wailing to all that he had left his life's savings, $2,600, in a shoe in Silver's Baths! Frenzy and confusion set in as family members lost each other, some clad only in towels, and all seeking to distance themselves from the clouds of fire and smoke leaping boldly above the stricken area.

On taking command of the fire-fighting, Patrick deployed his men so as to encircle the outer fringes of the blaze with their water streams, gradually moving in to smother the fire. Intense smoke reduced all vision and the heat was blistering. The encirclement began to work, the outer edges of the fire disappearing in smoke as the men advanced. Then, without warning, the antiquated high-pressure water system sputtered and failed, leaving small groups of firemen at the edge of the heat with pathetic streams of water trickling from their hoses. One high-pressure stream gave out just as it was trained on a half-dozen firemen entering a burning apartment building, leaving them without defense against the extreme heat.

It fell to Patrick to find the quickest way to regain water power. He lost no time in dispatching two fireboats to position themselves at 20th Street and Coney Island Creek to start pumping salt water into the system. His land-based pumpers then went to work transferring the low-pressure flow to the high-pressure system. The maneuver succeeded and by sundown that evening the fire had been extinguished. The devastation was contained within the original four blocks, and the rest of the vulnerable seaside colony stood unscratched. Published accounts of the Coney Island disaster mention that Walsh's attack on the fire was through a process of encirclement, directing a high-pressure flow of water at the flames from all sides. But through studying, observing and experimenting over the years, Patrick gradually departed from this traditional method. In contrast to the then-orthodox theory that the more hose lines trained on the blaze the better since the sheer volume of water was what counted, Patrick began to advocate attacking a fire exclusively from one side. Sending the water in the direction that the wind was blowing, the men under his command drove the fire ahead of the hose lines, beating down the flames and allowing a line of fire fighters to enter the building. He found this an economy of effort, both quicker and safer. The old method of encirclement, he maintained, tended to allow the fire to keep burning in the center of the building. By the time Patrick became chief of department, he was considered to have revolutionized fire-fighting methods.[2]

As assistant commissioner, Patrick could easily have cut back on the number of fires he personally covered. Regulations required him to respond to any fifth alarm fire in his district but most often he was there on the third alarm. It was never his style to remain standing on the fringe shouting commands. Finding a cluster of men hesitating on a fire escape he would quip, "Are you waiting for the fire to come to you, lads?" and he would lead the way in. If the smoke were heavy, he got down on his stomach and crawled, since breathable air was more likely found close to the ground.

One of Patrick's eyes had always been weak and, by the early 1930's, he hardly saw out of it at all. Mary Ann urged him to to stay out of burning buildings, fearing something might fall on the side of his bad eye and he would be slow in reacting. It was a caution Patrick never heeded.

Patrick's solid build, robust appearance and high levels of energy gave the impression of positive good health and such had generally been the case. But fire department personnel records document that, in 1933, he underwent surgery for ulcers and was hospitalized for several weeks. Whether or not the unacknowledged strains of his life brought about the ulcer condition cannot be answered. In any event, the fast pace he lived at was slowed to a halt for the space of the operation and its aftermath.

About this time, perhaps even during the period of his recuperation, Patrick read articles and talked to fire department colleagues who were enthusiastic about the possibilities of a recent innovation. New oil burners were becoming increasingly popular as home heating units in place of furnaces fired by coal. Patrick came to the conclusion that this could be a perfect line of business for son Jerry to enter, perhaps just the opportunity he needed. When Patrick was taken with an idea, action inevitably followed. He lost no time in placing a long-distance call to Lafayetteville, near Rhinebeck, New York, where Jerry and Betty were spending a brief vacation at a country house owned by Betty's sister. "Come home right away. We've got to talk about this."

Betty recalled her husband Jerry as the only one of Patrick's children who occasionally stood up to his father, answering him back at times when the others would have kept silent. Although she was typically deferential toward her father-in-law, there were episodes when she vented her feelings. Once, witnessing Patrick strike Joe in the face — Joe being twenty-two at the time and almost out of law school — she blurted out, "Don't you ever do that to Jerry." Patrick did not answer her.

Although on occasion Jerry resisted his father's autocratic ways, he did take the train down from Lafayetteville on a summer's day in 1933. He listened to Patrick reviewing the situation and, by the end of the summer, had quit his job at the IRT and gotten into the business of selling oil burners. During the following year, Betty remembered taking the subway with Jerry to the apartment on Joralemon Street so Jerry could report to his father at regular intervals on the progress of the business. At times Patrick glanced through the newspaper while Jerry was talking to him and offered no comment at the end of the briefing. One day Betty lost patience and exclaimed to Jerry, "How can you talk to a newspaper!" Again Patrick declined to acknowledge her comment.

Filial obedience, willingness, a good-faith effort, even his father's monetary investment were not sufficient for Jerry to succeed in the oil-burner business. Betty could see it coming on and by the end of a year it was also clear to Jerry that he was not cut out for self-employment, particularly in a line in which he had no technical knowledge or experience. The episode was upsetting to both Patrick and Jerry and placed further strain on their relationship.

Jerry reapplied for his job in the legal department of the IRT. But the economy was in the throes of the Depression, with municipal services in a holding pattern and every job opening oversubscribed. Jerry walked the streets during the next months filing job applications wherever he could. He even wrote a letter to President Franklin Roosevelt who, years before, had said to the young orderly aboard the *George Washington*: "If I can ever do anything for you, Jerry, just get in touch." It was a shot in the dark but there was no reply.

Finally the IRT advised that it had an opening, but it was not Jerry's former desk job. He would have to reenter the company as a subway conductor. This had little appeal but he was anxious to work and, after a year in the subways, he managed to get reinstated as an investigator in the legal department.

Although they longed for children, neither Jerry and Betty nor Joe and Mary were able to have them. The sons must have suffered for themselves but also in relation to Patrick's expectations. Probably little or nothing was ever said about this in the household, at least not directly to the couples, but words were not needed for the sons to perceive their father's disappointment.

Jerry and Betty had raised two of Betty's nephews in the mid-1920's, following the death of a sister. They had grown attached to the youngsters and would have liked to adopt them but that was not to be. After a few years, the brother-in-law remarried and took the boys away.

Unlike Patrick, Mary Ann did not worry about Jerry who was not as outwardly successful as his brothers. She knew her son was good-natured, generous and happy in his marriage to Betty. The settledness of the heart was what she valued.

But, as an Irish mother, Mary Ann could not help but take special pride in her two priest sons. She was clearly jubilant on that June day in 1934 when her youngest boy was ordained in Washington. Perhaps her happiness that day included an element of recognition that her work was, in a way, completed. She had given birth to ten children and the six who remained to her were each settled in his own chosen way.

The family had once again visited Ocean City in the summer of 1934. Paul was staying at the Dominican vacation house prior to receiving his first assignment as a priest. It was on the sidewalk in front of the tourist home in Ocean City that a picture was taken of a thinner, older Mary Ann. She had high blood pressure and had to watch her diet, but the weight loss had been more pronounced than expected.

Everyone noticed that Mary Ann continued to fail during the following winter. She was seventy-two and certainly had to slow down, take things easier, let others wait on her a bit instead of always being the one to serve. She agreed to see a doctor and stay under his care. She cooperated and paced herself more slowly.

May 4, 1935, was a Saturday. Mary Ann had an afternoon appointment with Dr. Schmidt whose office was on Sydney Place, directly opposite St. Charles church. Joe had picked Patrick up early that day to drive out to the Engineers' Club golf course in Roslyn, Long Island.

Events may have developed like this. The spring day was sunny and beckoning and Mary Ann gave herself ample time to stroll the few blocks to her three o-clock appointment. She had always loved spring. Her spirit was quickened by the quality of the sunlight, the bright green of the new leaves on the trees at curbside. Tulip bulbs were sprouting in many of the small front yards along Joralemon Street. Geranium shoots appeared in window boxes outside the tall first-floor windows of the brownstone houses. Robins were back in Brooklyn and hopped about listening for worms maneuvering beneath the surfaces of tiny lawns.

Taking careful steps, with a cane for support, Mary Ann moved down Joralemon Street. A parish friend called a greeting from a doorway across the street and Mary Ann waved the hand that held the square, black pocketbook. She liked to carry that purse which matched the round straw hat topping her bunned hair. Turning the corner at Sydney Place she arrived at Dr. Schmidt's office. "He's been called away on an emergency but should be back in a half hour," the nurse advised. Mary Ann decided to spend the half hour visiting the church across the street.

The normally dark interior of St. Charles was darker still when stepping into it from sunshine. She took a seat in a rear pew, engulfed in the stillness of that large space — a tangible space that appeared to be supported by the four rows of white stone pillars that lined the length of the interior. Above the altar, white statuary depicted the Crucifixion; above that was the huge, stained-glass window with a scene from the life of the Sixteenth Century Cardinal Charles Borromeo. Three or four other people were in the church. Mary Ann could hear the sound of rosaries tapping against the wood of the pews. An old lady sat nearby, probably unmindful that she was projecting syllables of the Hail Mary in hissed half tones.

Mary Ann took her rosary from her pocketbook and began to pray. Hail Mary, Holy Mary. Drowsiness set in and she nodded. Shaking herself, she decided to get up and make the Stations of the Cross. If only she got herself started, she would feel more energetic. Surely the Lord himself had no energy when he followed that first Via Crucis. She walked toward the main altar, stopping in the center aisle opposite the first station, Christ before Pilate. Gripping the top of the pew, she genuflected slowly. "We adore Thee, O Christ, and we bless Thee. Because by Thy holy Cross, Thou has redeemed the world." She moved along. Jesus falls the first time. Patrick inside burning buildings with one nearly blind eye. Michael now had five children. She named each of them to the Lord. Had Jerry's bronchial condition become worse?

Mary Ann continued along. Veronica wiped the Lord's face. Simon helped Him to carry His Cross. The women of Jerusalem wept over Him. The ninth station, Jesus falls the third time. "We adore Thee, O Christ." She began to genuflect but, instead of kneeling, her body crumpled and she sprawled out on the tile floor of the center aisle.

Joseph drove Patrick at breakneck speed the forty miles from Roslyn, but Mary Ann had been dead when they found her and lifted her from the floor of the church.

Mary Ann's death was the first tragic loss Patrick had to bear alone, without the support she had always been there to give. Eight years earlier, at their thirty-fifth wedding anniversary, he had toasted her with a poem that ended in these verses:

> But now the silver in our hair
>   Reminds us, Father Time,
> Is slowly coming on apace,
>   Yet, why should we repine
> For with our children we are blessed,
>   And thank the Lord on high,
> For all that He has given us,
>   While years kept rolling by.
> And, since the prime of life is past,
>   Now let us hand in hand
> March bravely down declining years,
>   Far from our native land;
> That, when the Lord will on us call,
>   Our spirits free may fly,
> To join our loved ones gone before
>   The years kept rolling by.

He might have felt somehow that, when the call came, it would be for both of them together, that their spirits would indeed have been the freest flying together.

Following the funeral, Patrick took several days to think and pray on his own at daughter Mary's Cenacle Retreat House on Long Island. Mary Ann's sudden death left each member of the family keenly aware of the role the mother had played at the center of their close-knit group. The Saturday night gatherings continued only intermittently. When they did meet, it was easier to go to Michael's house or Joe's house where one of the wives prepared a meal. Mary Ann had supplied the atmosphere of home at the Joralemon Street apartment even though the sons had never actually lived there. Probably no one had spelled out for himself the meaning of her presence, but each was overwhelmed by the suddenness of her absence.

CHAPTER TEN

Catapulted to the Top

1936 - 1940

 An article published in a 1936 fire department journal featured the senior Assistant Fire Chief this way:

At sixty-three years of age,* he is hale and hearty, a robust, rugged figure who entered the service for excitement and today, after thirty-five years at it, still enjoys it. It is his very life, especially now that his wife is gone. He has five jewels of children, two priests, two lawyers and a girl in a convent.[1]

One wonders why Jerry was not counted as the sixth jewel. Certainly Patrick never said to anyone that he had five children rather than six. But since it came to him naturally to boast of the lawyers, the priests and the nun, a listener assumed that such was the sum of his family.

The same magazine article has another remarkable observation: "One of the proudest accomplishments is that he never had to take a day of sick leave on the force." If such a statement could be printed in a fire department publication then it would appear that even fire officials with whom Patrick interacted on a daily basis were not aware he had undergone an operation for ulcers three years earlier. Perhaps he had chosen to assign that absence to vacation rather than sick leave so his health problem would not be known. Perhaps the robust and vigorous Patrick Walsh was an image that could not be tampered with, a myth or ideal that would be betrayed by any evidence of weakness. Patrick felt compelled to be a model and

---

* Sixty-eight in actual years.

maintain the highest standards for the sake of his family and also for the sake of the fire department toward which he felt paternal devotion. This model he sought to embody might have been all the more persuasive had he acknowledged and integrated his own human limitations. But such was not Patrick's thinking. His heroes were untainted.

Shortly after this article's publication, Patrick experienced his closest brush with death. Early in the morning of March 12, 1936, the assistant chief hurried to the scene of a large fire that was engulfing a warehouse in a shipyard in South Brooklyn. He and Battalion Chief Anthony Jireck had climbed the stairs to the second floor just before a backdraft sent scores of fire fighters scurrying out of the building to safety. There was general concern when Walsh and Jireck did not emerge as well. Concern turned to horror when the only stairway began to crumble. Then suddenly Patrick appeared on the roof, signaling for a ladder. He and Jireck scampered down the eighty-five feet only moments before the roof gave way. It was a very close call.

On June 12, 1936, the daily newspaper the *New York Telegram* featured Patrick in one of a series of six articles on "Famous Firemen." "Square-faced, laconic Patrick J. Walsh is an oldtime fireman, one of the hard-boiled men responsible for making this city's Fire Department the most efficient in the world." After summarizing the chief's fire department and personal histories it commented: "The Fire Department and the Roman Catholic Church are his only interests. He is uncommonly religious."

Father Paul Walsh recalled that, in the year or two following his mother's death, Patrick did indeed become uncommonly religious. He started attending two masses instead of one every morning at St. Charles, the second in Mary Ann's memory, celebrated in the very sanctuary where she had died.

He also became increasingly obsessed with questions of a religious nature. Sometime in 1936, Patrick visited son Jack at his priory in Somerset, Ohio. The priory included a substantial library and Patrick installed himself at one of its tables for the space of several days. Piling up books in front of him including most of the eighteen volumes of the *Catholic Encyclopedia*, he read with close attention and took notes. One weighty treatise that particularly interested him was Josephus' "History of the Jews." Why had God's chosen people not recognized Jesus Christ as the promised Messiah? What was the ultimate destiny of the Jews? Although he found no clear answers to these unanswerable questions, he continued to read and ponder.

By the end of 1937, the family was clearly concerned about how he spent so much time alone in his apartment, that his spirits were not as buoyant as usual and that he was no longer eating properly. They convinced him to hire a maid who came each day to straighten the apartment and prepare his supper. Neighbors in the parish, who had known the family for years, would occasionally drop by. A few of daughter Mary's old friends were among those who called. One of them remembers that the girls abruptly stopped visiting when they heard a vapid comment bandied about the neighborhood that Chief Walsh was receiving young women in his apartment.

It is unclear if the idea was initially Patrick's or if one of the sons planted the suggestion. Three years after Mary Ann's death, Patrick went to Hartford, Connecticut, to bring back a second wife. Anne Connors was a widow, fifty-six years old and some fourteen years younger than he. She was originally part of the Ryan family from Tipperary, a cousin of Mary Ann's. Patrick and Annie, as everyone called her, were married by Father Paul at a private ceremony attended by the immediate family at St. Charles church in August, 1938.

Annie was a very different personality from her cousin. Mary Ann had been the quintessential mother, even extending her motherly ways toward her husband. She had been the one who waited on people, preferring to keep herself in the background. Annie never had children of her own and had no inclination to assume a motherly role toward Patrick's grown family. She gave priority to being wife and companion to the assistant chief, and was willing to pursue cooking and housekeeping in the traditions set by Mary Ann. Annie entered Patrick's life at a time when he would increasingly be called upon to attend social events, dinners and ceremonies where the presence of a wife was helpful and appropriate. Mary Ann would have shied away from such functions. Annie had a clear sense of herself, an outgoing personality and a ready sense of humor. Her high-pitched laughter might have seemed affected to those who scarcely knew her.

Michael's children have only fond memories of "Aunt Annie' who always treated them with interest and good humor. However, the daughters-in-law, Catherine, Betty and Mary Bergen, hardly received their new mother-in-law with glad hearts. Catherine objected to second marriages in general, which to her implied faithlessness to the memory of the precious, shared history with the original partner. Annie had appeared on the scene out of nowhere to take up the role of the chief's wife and companion. Her bubbly personality irked the younger wives who made fun among themselves of her Irish brogue and, particularly, the tilt of her head and her obvious enjoyment of her new status. As is common within Irish families, the outer relationships among the members were always cordial and proper. The "day after" comments that sang along the telephone lines were more telling.

The wedding in August, 1938, lingered only briefly at the center of family attention. New York State held its gubernatorial election in November, bringing victory to the incumbent Democrat Herbert H. Lehman. Edward J. Flynn, the secretary of state who served through Lehman's earlier terms, resigned. In the ethnically balanced politics of New York State, the governor needed an Irish Catholic to replace him and Michael Walsh was his designee.

Michael Francis Walsh was his father's son. As the oldest, his father's influence on him had been strongest. Church and family were supremely important to Michael. Like Patrick he was competitive and driven to achieve within his career. Although his personality required the confirmation of tangible success, his aim was not personal aggrandizement. That inbred need of father and son to do and be the best in a chosen field was highly purposeful. Doing one's best was directed to serving God, Church and Community. For Michael, as for Patrick, life's efforts had real meaning only in that context.

New York Secretary of State Michael Walsh,
circa 1941.
Mike was often a guest speaker at public functions.

Michael's public activity began when he joined the Catholic fraternal organization, the Knights of Columbus, as a young lawyer just prior to his marriage in 1919. Serious and willing to devote his time, he rose to positions of statewide leadership as a state deputy and then Supreme Director.

The Knights of Columbus, dedicated to upholding and defending the position of the Catholic church within a Protestant/secular society, were concerned that public policy should enhance rather than impede the church's interests. Many public issues had direct relevance to Catholics: aid to parochial schools, the relaxation of divorce laws, the treatment of pornography, Communist infiltration into government, and so on. With his talents as a lawyer, Michael proved a natural leader in the organization. As the Knights of Columbus state advocate in 1930, he participated in the Harriman schoolteacher case — upholding the right of a Catholic to teach in public schools. In 1935, as Knights of Columbus state deputy, he initiated the movement for legislation to provide bus transportation for parochial school children. As a Catholic organization within the political arena, the Knights of Columbus of that time sought to achieve its goals through the Democratic party. Many of the Democratic district leaders in the state were Irish Catholics who either sympathized with the aims of the Knights or recognized the political feasibility of showing support.

It was against this background of public leadership that Michael, in 1937, was appointed a commissioner of the Port of New York Authority. His brother Paul maintains that it was Michael who named the Lincoln Tunnel. When the commissioners were asked for their suggestions about what to call the newly terminated conduit between Forty-Second Street, Manhattan and Union City, New Jersey, it was supposedly Michael who said when his turn came around: "Gentlemen, we already have the George Washington Bridge why not now the Abraham Lincoln Tunnel?" An original tile from the tunnel with "Commissioner Michael F. Walsh - May 20, 1937" printed on the back, is still a family possession.

In May, 1938, Michael was appointed by President Roosevelt to serve as United States Attorney for the Eastern District of New York. He held the post for less than a year, resigning when he received Governor Lehman's invitation to be secretary of state.

As Michael's activities increased within civic and religious forums, he was often invited as guest speaker at public functions. He was never one to deliver a speech "off the cuff." Any address he gave was a chance to educate his audience which, to him, required his thought, research and the crafting of the text. Much of his preparation happened in his den at home in the small hours of the morning while his family slept. A favorite topic for speeches was the responsibility of the Catholic layman under the guidance of the hierarchy; another was the natural law as the source of American democracy. The bishop of Brooklyn often called on Michael for assistance and advice and Cardinal Francis J. Spellman of New York kept in contact with him.

Michael resembled his father in that the political world as such did not interest him. He never felt the urge to run for public office. He possessed an even temperament, was open and accessible to people, and friends encouraged him to think in terms of politics. A short-lived rumor circulated that he would be a candidate for New York City mayor in 1940, but Michael had never given this a serious thought.

For all the time Michael gave to public affairs, he seemed happiest when he was home in the company of Catherine and his five children. Frank and Jack were in high school, Mary, Kathleen and Patricia in elementary school. Whenever his schedule allowed, he spent his Sundays on family outings. After Mass and breakfast he piled the younger ones into the car for an afternoon at Prospect Park Zoo or the Coney Island boardwalk, allowing "Kitty," as he called his wife, to have some time for herself at home. Friends recalled that at a July 4th celebration at a fashionable country club on Long Island, when the party was at its peak, Michael made his apologies and departed with Catherine, having promised his children he would be home to set off evening fireworks. It was no small sacrifice that Michael had to attend so many social functions, spend so much time in Albany, participate in Knights of Columbus trips, or attend local meetings. A sense of responsibility, rather than a natural gusto, seemed to propel him through much of his activities. Michael was always in touch with Pop. The two were genuine friends. Michael had been able to weather Patrick's discipline and move beyond it to an adult relationship of mutual regard. Michael telephoned his father regularly and arranged to have lunch with him whenever their schedules permitted. Any holiday brought the family together and Mike, always running a little behind time, rushed over to Brooklyn Heights to drive Patrick (and later Patrick and Annie) home to Flatbush for dinner. Michael's East Nineteenth Street home was now the place where the family congregated. Betty and Jerry came, as did Joe and Mary Bergen. Fathers Jack and Paul, if on assignment in the area, never missed family dinner on a holiday.

The long-standing rituals continued. As soon as the dishes were cleared, the Setback game began at the dining-room table. Those who took cards seriously wanted quiet, but Patrick was always reluctant to conclude a debate with his lawyer sons on whatever current topic arose during dinner. Although daughter Mary, at her cloistered convent in Lake Ronkonkoma, was never part of these gatherings, her ties to the family were as close as ever. Everyone did his best to visit her once a month.

In December, 1938, when the elation over Michael's appointment as secretary of state had hardly subsided, Patrick was stricken again with bleeding ulcers and was hospitalized for six weeks.

Perhaps worry over Jerry's deteriorating health contributed to this ulcer attack. By 1937 Jerry and Betty were no longer coming to Sunday gatherings. Jerry's bronchial condition had worsened so much that he was forced to seek a disability retirement from the IRT. By 1938 he seldom got out of bed.

Betty was convinced Jerry's decline began during the year he spent in the subway tunnels of the IRT, that the dank environment was the worst possible for his chronic condition. In Betty's mind, the phone call from Patrick to Lafayetteville in the summer of 1933 urging Jerry to switch to the oil-burner business was the beginning of the

132/ LaGuardia's Fire Chief

end for her husband. She also felt the doctors never clearly diagnosed Jerry's illness. He had spit up blood during the last three years, a symptom not usually associated with a generalized bronchial condition. Jerry died in February, 1940, at the age of forty-three. Even though the long sickness and his gradually declining state had prepared the family for the inevitable, his death was a blow. It is impossible to know if Patrick felt at all implicated in Jerry's fate. Betty's interpretation of what happened in the 1930's was her personal version. Familiarity with Patrick's ways and blind spots would lead one to guess that he truly grieved for Jerry but felt no guilt at having been a disturbing agent in his life.

Maybe Patrick had Jerry in mind some four years later when he spoke at a department memorial service. "Sorrow for the dead is the only sorrow from which we refuse to be divorced," he said, and urged his listeners to be "more faithful and more affectionate to those that are living."[2]

Jerry Walsh was buried next to his mother in Holy Cross cemetery in Brooklyn on February 21, 1940. Two days later Patrick was appointed acting Chief of the New York City Fire Department.

As is the case in the police department, the fire department has two executive officers, chief and commissioner. The chief is the top job of the uniformed fire-fighting force, serving directly under the commissioner. The chief must be a fireman by profession, one who has come up through the ranks in successive civil service examinations. He directly manages fire-fighting operations throughout the city and sometimes personally takes command at the scene of significant fires. The commissioner, on the other hand, is the administrator, the one who oversees the total organization, who ensures the structure is such that goals are met successfully and efficiently. The commissioner may be drafted from an entirely different field of work and may never have witnessed a fire in his life. The two jobs call for two different sets of skills.

Throughout New York City Fire Department history the top positions were filled by separate individuals. But Mayor LaGuardia thought differently and preferred to draw his administrator from the fire-fighting ranks. At the start of LaGuardia's first term in January, 1934, he had appointed the then Fire Chief John J. McElligott as commissioner. Patrick served as first assistant to McElligott for those six years. In February, 1940, McElligott decided to retire from his chief position and continue only as commissioner. Thus LaGuardia named Patrick acting chief, or head of the uniformed firemen responsible for the fire protection of the city. Patrick had held the rank of assistant chief since 1926. Now his career was on the rise again.

CHAPTER ELEVEN

World War II and Fiorello LaGuardia

1940 - 1942

 New York is a blasé metropolis that believes it has seen everything. Yet the incongruous Fiorello LaGuardia hit the city like a thunderbolt. The fact he was the son of immigrants gave him an authentic link to the melting pot center of America. But everything else was different about the man who bounded up the steps of City Hall to be inaugurated as mayor of New York City in January, 1934. He was an Italian-American Protestant of half-Jewish descent. In a city governed predominantly by Democrats, with Republicans the only sizable opposition, he was elected on a fusion or nonpartisan ticket with only forty percent of the popular vote.

Nor did LaGuardia's physical appearance resemble anybody's concept of a mayor. He was five-foot-three inches in height, round and overweight. The voice, which tended to a falsetto, was given to ranting and raving, producing a crescendo that penetrated the closed doors of his office and echoed down the marble corridors of City Hall. A dynamo of energy, he propelled himself about the city in a crumpled suit and oversized fedora hat. No one knew where the mayor would make his next appearance. He might show up at a shelter for the homeless, talking with the indigents lined up at the door, or descend upon a police precinct to mete out punishment personally to arrested gamblers. One December morning before daylight he arrived at The Bronx Terminal Market, scrambled up on the tailboard of a truck and announced his assault on racketeers in the artichoke business. In a completely different setting, the elegant Carnegie Hall, he conducted a special performance of the Sanitation

Department band (after instructing a stage manager to "just treat me like Toscanini").[1]

He had entered the mayoral office as would a fighter to a ring. "No more free lunch," was his promise. The politicos and reporters who milled about City Hall the morning of his inauguration smiled benignly and skeptically, but LaGuardia had every intention of acting on his words. As an initial measure in the balancing of a bloated city budget, he slashed thousands of nonessential jobs from the payroll and reduced salaries of many employees who remained.[2]

The Fusion Conference Committee had coalesced in a crusade to thwart domination by Tammany Hall Democrats and bring honest and efficient government to the City of New York. Through the 1920's, a period when the standards of many businessmen were not appreciably higher than those of machine politicians, people seemed less inclined to show concern about Tammany activities in city government.[3] But the Depression had put a new perspective on things. In the period 1929-1932, New York City became the subject of an intense investigation into corruption. Spearheaded by Judge Samuel Seabury, the investigating commission revealed how the administration of Tammany's Mayor Jimmy Walker had siphoned off hundreds of thousands of dollars from the city treasury into the pockets of a handful of city officials and their private business contacts. The 1931 disclosure that Tammany politicians had utilized a ten million-dollar relief fund to fuel the campaigns of party members scandalized and outraged even jaded New Yorkers. Mayor Walker resigned and sailed for Paris in 1932. The anger felt by voters at the extent of the corruption, especially in the context of the Great Depression, had paved the way for a Reform victory in the mayoral elections of 1933.

Fiorello LaGuardia, himself raised in tenements, showed genuine compassion for the city's underprivileged. To many he was a New Dealer before the New Deal. The fact he also shouted and raged and was not above bullying people caused one municipal official to remark, "He's a son-of-a-bitch, but you believe what he's doing is right."[4]

The Depression served LaGuardia's administration in one particular respect. Since businesses had failed all over the city and unemployment was soaring, government service found a pool of capable young men who in better times would not have sought jobs in the municipal bureaucracy. The civil service reforms LaGuardia put into effect for the selection of manpower on the basis of merit rather than political connection brought a new professionalism into city government which did much to raise its prestige.[5]

But LaGuardia's personality often put him at odds with the very professionals he sought to attract. The mayor wanted things done *his* way and had small regard for independent judgment, let alone independent action. Rexford Tugwell, Planning Commission chairman, recalled with chagrin: "He boasted to newspapers of his appointees. . . . He did not say that he often treated his commissioners like dogs. . . ."[6]

Robert A. Caro presents a graphic picture of what Mr. Tugwell was referring to:

> The Mayor moved his desk to the far end of his thirty-two-foot-long office so that visitors would have a longer walk to reach him, and when a commissioner entered — usually after a long heel-cooling period outside — the Mayor would often further unnerve him by covering his face with his fingers and peering between them so that, as the commissioner approached, all he could see of his boss's face was a pair of button-bright little eyes staring at him. A commissioner who displeased LaGuardia by inefficiency — or by showing even a hint of independence — would be abused as if he were a wayward child. And the abuse was not delivered only in private: in his desk the Mayor kept a large bronze bone and at intervals he would call his commissioners together so that in front of them all he could "award" it to the one who had pulled the biggest recent boner; once, with a commissioner in his office, the Mayor summoned a secretary and berated her viciously for an imaginary mistake — just so that he could have the pleasure of concluding the tirade by shouting, "If you were any dumber, I'd make you a commissioner." Many commissioners resigned; the turnover in the LaGuardia administration, Tugwell says, "must have been unprecedented in municipal history.[7]

(The one commissioner with whom LaGuardia could not

have his way was the regal Robert Moses, head of the Parks Department. The tug of war between two strong-willed men has been well documented and Moses was one of the few survivors of LaGuardia's twelve years in office.)

Until 1937 it had been an iron law of New York City history that a reform administration never succeeded itself. LaGuardia again was the exception. Although the Republicans now reluctantly backed his candidacy, the incumbent won overwhelmingly with 1,344,630 votes to the Democratic candidate's 890,756. Whatever the people thought of his excesses, he had convinced them that he stood for honest government and possessed the clout to get things done.

The re-election fanfare of 1937 had hardly subsided in New York City when Fiorello LaGuardia began to cast his eyes toward an even higher calling. Franklin Delano Roosevelt would not be likely to pursue a third term in 1940; no American president had done so. The stage seemed open to newcomers and why not to a maverick who had proven himself capable of governing the largest and most ungovernable of American cities? The first two years of his second term, LaGuardia seriously entertained this possibility and courted every opportunity for national exposure. But the advance of Hitler's armies in March of 1940 generated the type of national alarm that forced the issue of "no third term" into obscurity. Continuity seemed a necessary ingredient of security. LaGuardia acquiesced to the wave of support for Roosevelt's presidential reelection and proceeded to make plans to prolong his own tenure in New York. If a third term for a chief executive was all right for the country, it would be all right for its largest city also. After all, New York was "the logical, most attractive and tempting target for a foreign enemy."[8]

It remained to be seen whether New Yorkers would agree with LaGuardia's assessment of his own indispensability to the city's survival. Certainly he would hope to run again in the city election of November, 1941, on his record of honest government. In this light, the mayor could ill afford politically the revelations of graft within the city's fire department headlined in the press in April of election year.

The Department of Investigation had charged six firemen assigned to oil-burner inspections with shaking down businessmen for undercover fees. In the case of fireman Albert Becker, eighteen witnesses had attested that the defendant had exacted small gratuities from them. However, Trial Commissioner George McKenna, a deputy in the fire department, found Becker not guilty of accepting gratuities but at the same time fined him thirty day's pay for conduct unbecoming a city employee. LaGuardia immediately reacted by ousting Deputy Commissioner McKenna from office and then asking for the resignation of Fire Commissioner John McElligott. According to the *New York Times,* the mayor alleged, "I am very fond of McElligott and I hated to have to do it. . . . He approved of the findings which is contrary to my policy of keeping petty grafters out of the service." "McElligott Ousted with Chief Deputy over Graft Trials," read first column headlines of May 9, 1941. "Walsh Gets Post."

A fire department newspaper commented that there had not been such a shake-up in the department since Chief Croker's ouster in 1902. The columnist added that "out of the upheaval came the smiling countenance of the amiable Assistant Fire Chief Paddy Walsh as the new Fire Commissioner."[9]

Chances are that Patrick Walsh never expected a turn at being commissioner of the New York City Fire Department, with sole responsibility for a corps of 11,000 uniformed and civilian employees. Although acting chief since February of 1940, he was never certain he would be named permanent chief, let alone contemplate the commissionership. McElligott, several years Patrick's junior and LaGuardia's commissioner since the mayor took office in 1934, had successfully survived the ups and downs of close association with his vitriolic boss. Since McElligott was the first commissioner in fire department history to be appointed from the fireman ranks and serve both as chief and commissioner, the chances of a subsequent mayor repeating that move were slim; and, of course, if LaGuardia continued as mayor for a third term, McElligott might well continue along with him. But no one could have predicted the revelations of graft and LaGuardia's immediate charge on his white steed of honesty. Patrick was catapulted to the top office from one day to the next.

*The Mayor and Commissioner Walsh touch base
with members of Rescue 1 at a World War II drill*

The newspaper photograph taken at the official swearing-in ceremony the day after McElligott was ousted shows a grim-looking LaGuardia receiving the oath of office from a full-faced, smiling, spectacled Patrick. The new commissioner's head is bald, save for a tonsure-like rim of hair around the back of the scalp. The square frame of his body is now decidedly stocky. Michael and Catherine stand behind him at his left, while grandson Frank, at six feet, looms over his shoulders. A demure-looking Annie, with her flowered straw hat, flanks him to the right and next to her, completing the picture, is a giggly granddaughter, Mary, a few days short of her eleventh birthday. Mary, when in her fifties, clearly remembered feeling properly squelched when the picture was received and one of the adults (Aunt Annie?) accused her of offending the solemnity of the occasion. But the newspaper account of the event seems to indicate that the new commissioner felt rather giddy that day, along with his granddaughter. The *New York Times* reported:

> From the Mayor's large room Commissioner Walsh went to an adjoining office room, signed the "oath book" and paid the prescribed 6 cents to Arthur Walker, chief clerk of the Mayor's office.
> The Commissioner went to his office in the Municipal Building only for a short time and then left for the rest of the day. He said he had completed his tour of duty at 8 o'clock in the morning.
> He was smiling happily as he posed for photographers with his hat on and off, his glasses on and off, and kissing his granddaughter Mary.[10]

The newspaper summed up the new commissioner's response to the swearing-in ceremony as "Walsh Pledges His Better-Than-Best." "Your Honor, I deeply appreciate the honor you have conferred on me this morning. It is far more than I deserve. I have always done the best I could in the department, but I hope now to do better than ever. I couldn't do much alone, but I believe I've got the confidence of the officers and men of the department."

LaGuardia remarked simply, "There is nothing any Mayor can

tell you about the Fire Department. I won't try."[11]

The mayor knew quite a bit about Patrick Walsh and liked what he saw. Patrick's reputation as an honest, hard-working, religious family man supported the image that LaGuardia sought to project in his administration. A commentator in *The Chief* wrote that if Walsh found "any graft or 'take,' the guilty ones will 'walk the plank.' He can look any man right in the eye and tell him where to get off, because you can't compromise him."[12] Patrick respected authority and was hardly likely to challenge LaGuardia's direction. The mayor knew Walsh would not seek personal power or political mileage from his office. He would be a commissioner who would probably not give him much occasion to rant and rave. And after eight years in office, LaGuardia might have mellowed somewhat in this respect.

In conformity with instructions from Mayor LaGuardia, Patrick as commissioner transferred himself from acting Chief to official Chief of Department. As in the case of McElligott, the two jobs would be held by one man. Since Patrick had served as acting chief during the preceding year, the Municipal Civil Service Commission amended its rules to allow him to become permanent chief even though he had not taken the usual civil service examination for the position. The Chief Officers' Association voiced opposition to this departure from the traditional rule but the move was judged legal and the appointment held.[13] The focus of the resentment must have centered in the ranks of the department's fifty-four deputy chiefs who would have been eligible to compete for Chief of Department had an examination been given.

If there existed any area of friction between Mayor LaGuardia and his fire commissioner, it would have had to deal with LaGuardia's penchant for making personal appearances at fires. One biographer claims the mayor had never lost the small boy's thrill at following an engine to the site of a fire.[14] Hearing LaGuardia talk about a fire he had witnessed was clear indication of how strongly he identified with fire fighting. In a speech at a department awards ceremony, he gave a vivid description of blazing flames aboard a munitions ship in New York Bay. A fireboat had been dispatched from the Battery in lower Manhattan.

> . . . the commander gave the order and the fire fighter approached. It was hot there for a few minutes. It was tough. Every pound of steam that that ship could develop was thrown into those boilers. The fireboat quivered as it approached the gunwales of the *Estaro*. Thousands of tons of water under its decks. Oh, your city would have been proud of you had they been able to see it. That was a dramatic moment and we did put the fire out.

Then the mayor seemed to come out of his reverie. "I say 'we,' — let them laugh that off!"[15]

Given Patrick's old competitiveness about fires dating from the days of "one platoon," it was common knowledge that he did his utmost to edge the mayor out and arrive first at the scene. But the conflict between the two never developed beyond banter.

A common sight at a major fire were the figures of Walsh and LaGuardia on the sidewalk, side by side, hands on hips, one under a fire chief's helmet and the other a broad-brimmed Stetson, gazing up at a burning floor and assessing the fire's vital statistics. On one such occasion a couple of insurance adjusters entered the basement of a burning building to examine the situation firsthand. Patrick caught sight of them and let out an expletive but, before he could move, the short figure of the mayor at his side darted off and plunged into the building. Patrick followed closely behind to evict them all.[16]

On another occasion Walsh and LaGuardia stood on a pier off Battery Park observing a city fireboat doing battle with a blaze aboard a ship:

> LaGuardia: Let's go out to join them.
> Walsh: Those firemen are doing everything that can be done. We can go if you insist, but wouldn't be helping out and it might be distracting.

They stayed on the pier.[17]

But the fire chief/commissioner was seldom seen at a fire in the role of an observer. Although as chief he was only expected to arrive at a five-alarm fire, he made an effort to attend every three-alarm that

The fire extinguished, the Mayor and Walsh
exchange views.

broke out in any part of the five boroughs. His office on the eleventh floor of the Municipal Building was equipped with a bell similar to that in any fire house.

A "Profile" in the *New Yorker* magazine of April, 1942, described Walsh's behavior at the fires he attended:

> Occasionally, when his car pulls up at the scene, the Chief ...lands running at full tilt and disappears without preliminary into the burning edifice. Sometimes he pauses briefly to pick up a hose en route. He emerges every five or ten minutes to issue orders. Walsh is able to size up a fire almost instantly, and his decisions are greatly respected by his men. . . .
>
> There was recently a fire whose exact location in a rambling building was still unknown to the firemen at the time the Chief arrived. Smoke was pouring out all of the windows and the firemen, wheezing and gasping, were directing streams of water at the facade. As usual, Walsh disappeared from the public view upon arrival. Five minutes later, his round, ruddy, steel-bespectacled countenance was thrust out of a sixth-story window and his modulated voice floated down to the busy gathering below. "Lads," he said, "would you mind coming up here with a hose and putting out the fire?"[18]

Shortly after he was made commissioner, a serious fire occurred in the Hegeman Building housing a Modell's sporting-goods store at Broadway and Fulton Street. Other commitments that day had kept Patrick from responding. But when word reached him that a fireman had been killed in the blaze, he immediately left his engagement and hurried to the scene. That week's issue of *The Chief* included the following:

> When Commissioner Walsh arrived at the fire last Saturday following the finding of Fireman Bischoff's body, a policeman stopped him at the fire lines. "I'm the Fire Commissioner," said he softly. "You'll have to show me," said the cop and Chief Walsh did, while smilingly complimenting the officer on his efficiency.[19]

The fire had gutted the six-story Hegeman Building, a landmark dating from 1902. Curiously enough, the building that had stood on the same spot had also been destroyed by fire, on the night of December 11, 1901. That had been Patrick Walsh's second night in the fire department and his first fire.

The whole of Patrick's service as commissioner was dominated by one reality, the menace of World War II. Fear of a mammoth conflagration from bombing or sabotage pervaded New York City throughout the war, and the responsibility for meeting such an emergency was primarily in the hands of the city's fire commissioner.

Whatever the enemy had in mind, New Yorkers were convinced their own harbor would be a first-strike target. Hermann Goering, Hitler's second in command, later confirmed that a super V-2 robot bomb, capable of a rocket stratospheric trip to New York City, was nearing completion when D-Day in Normandy left the project at a standstill.

New York City's fire department had had an early contact with war preparations when Commander A.N. Firebrace of the London Fire Brigade spent the fall of 1936 visiting his New York counterparts. London was gearing up for a possible bombardment from Germany and thought to improve the level of effectiveness of its fire-fighting forces by a close-up study of how a city like New York organized its fire personnel and mechanical equipment. In 1936 most New Yorkers were viewing Hitler as the problem of another continent. However, in November, 1939, two months after war had broken out in Europe, LaGuardia established a War Protection Commission in New York City which included the fire commissioner and other selected city officials. They were to think the unthinkable. The fire department launched research aimed at identifying and expanding resources in areas vital to the survival of a city under attack: emergency communications systems, auxiliary sources of water, protection of an extensive waterfront. A marine plan involved the use of tugs and other harbor craft as an auxiliary arm of the fireboat fleet. Motorcycle dispatch riders and amateur radio operators were organized into a network to substitute in crises for a disrupted fire-alarm telegraph system.

By the time Hitler sent his armies across Europe in 1940, the threat of war had become real to the millions on the other side of the Atlantic. In January, 1941, New York sent three firemen to London, this time to be welcomed by Commander Firebrace. The three spent two months in England-at-war, joining British firemen on the trucks that raced to fires in the midst of severe bombardments by German planes. The officers survived to return to New York and give their own department a jolt as to what war was really like and what one day might be demanded of their own fire-fighting force. New York would have even greater problems, they emphasized, since it was a city of skyscrapers, while a building taller than six stories was a rarity in London.

In 1941 the mayor designated the fire commissioner as Fire Defense Coordinator for the city administration. If America entered the war, a marked increase could be expected in the number of fires stemming from sabotage, hostile attacks from the air, or accidents brought on by increased harbor traffic. The port of New York dominated the shipping industry of the whole eastern seaboard — fifty percent of the volume and seventy-five percent of the value of shipping goods came through New York harbor. From Far Rockaway in Queens to Pelham Bay in The Bronx, New York City encompassed five hundred and seventy-eight miles of waterfront. During the German bombing blitz, London had experienced ten thousand fires in one night. London's buildings and docks were of stone, while New York City in the 1940's had an abundance of wooden structures. Estimates classified a mere one-and-a-half percent of New York's buildings as reliably fireproof. Patrick was confident his department was equipped for peacetime defense against fires. But how could it respond on the scale that war might demand?

The single biggest innovation launched by Patrick in response to the threat of war on the homefront was the establishment of a Fire Department Emergency Auxiliary Corps.[20] The prospect appealed to Patrick's imagination — to organize and train a huge cadre of volunteer firemen as an emergency backup for the uniformed forces.

Challenge number one was selling the idea to the public. Firemen were selected and given a crash training course in public speaking to prepare them for addressing religious, political, fraternal and social organizations to plead for enrollment. Press and radio publicized the new auxiliaries and fire trucks toured the city with loudspeaker advertisements. Hundreds of thousands of pamphlets and handbills were distributed and signs posted in store windows, on subways and in buses.

Membership in this brand new auxiliary was limited to men in the eighteen to fifty-five age bracket and the race was on to recruit all able-bodied males who, for one reason or another, would not be subject to the draft. Special groups were singled out as likely recruitment sources: civil service employees, college students, retired firemen. In a communique to heads of all city departments, Commissioner Walsh requested lists of all employees who had not been classified 1A by the Selective Service. Cooperation from private business owners was sought in encouraging their employees to volunteer.

Such concentrated recruitment brought results and training these volunteers became the next crucial issue. Seventeen hundred officers of the department attended a ten-day course at New York University to prepare them for the instruction of these vast numbers of citizen-auxiliaries. A special training syllabus was drawn up with a sixty-hour core curriculum, supplemented by many hours of on-site demonstration of fire department equipment in operation. Fire company quarters throughout the city were utilized as training centers. The response was so great that many of the fire stations found themselves short of seats on the first night of instruction. One enterprising captain in Brooklyn ran out and borrowed six-dozen chairs from a neighboring undertaker.[21]

Training completed, an auxiliary was kept in shape through Saturday drills and periodic call-ups for refresher courses. Those physically fit were allowed to ride trucks to fires where they helped to stretch hose lines and connect hoses to pumps and hydrants. Others filled in as radio dispatchers or assisted in building inspections.

In August of 1941 a five-alarm fire broke out on Pier 27 of the Brooklyn waterfront. Patrick rushed to the scene and assessed the extent of the fire along with its potential for worsening. The wind was blowing from land to water but could reverse itself in an instant. The fire had to be blown out into the bay, and in a hurry. Walsh set about ordering the water pressure turned up but fire hoses spewing 175 liquid pounds became problematic for handling. Sighting the longshoremen lined up along the piers watching, the chief called for their help in steadying the dancing hose lines. The tactic worked and the fire was driven out into the water. A relieved Patrick thanked the volunteers who had helped to save Brooklyn that day.[22]

The inferno on Pier 27 had caused the movement of one-fifth of all the fire department's apparatus. "That's for *one* fire," said the mayor. "What would we do in the case of air raids or sabotage? Our present neutrality is fast diminishing."[23]

But by the time of Pearl Harbor in December, the mayor was sounding a note of confidence, at least for public consumption:

> The Fire Department is hitting on all cylinders. The precautionary work has been done quietly but the Department has displayed admirable ingenuity in creating and constructing special types of apparatus without additional cost to the City. . . . This stands out in splendid contrast to the system of thinking of an appropriation first and doing the job afterwards.[24]

At the time of the Pearl Harbor attack, New York's fire auxiliaries numbered 31,209. When amateurs assist professionals, especially in an area as intense as firefighting, the cooperation can be an uneasy one. In May of 1942 the national director of the Office of Civilian Defense, in a major address at a convention in Atlantic City, New Jersey, charged cities of the eastern seaboard with creating auxiliary fire-fighting forces that amounted to mere paper organizations. The OCD director cited jealousy between the pros and the volunteers. Professionals objected to the auxiliaries' use of department equipment, even for training purposes.

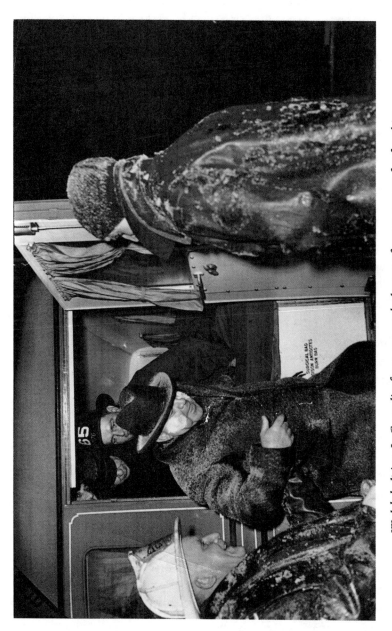

Walsh helping LaGuardia from an ambulance after treatment for frostbite.
A fire erupted at Pier 83 on the Hudson River in January, 1942, while temperatures hovered near zero.

Patrick bristled at the accusation. After all, he was chief of the largest auxiliary force in the country and certainly, in his opinion, the most effective. Such comments "reflect on the splendid work auxiliaries have done here," ran the quote by Patrick in the *New York Times*. And, further, if New York City had not used its own equipment but decided to wait for the Office of Civilian Defense to supply it, the auxiliaries would be using "baby carriages instead of regulation 85-foot aerial ladders and 1,000-gallon pumpers."[25]

But could there be some grounds for such a criticism by the OCD director? Patrick shot out telegrams of inquiry to fire chiefs in twenty of the larger cities along the eastern seaboard requesting that replies be wired back to him collect. Twenty answers arrived the next day. They read, "No jealousy in Hoboken," "No jealousy in Savannah," "No jealousy in Bangor," etc.[26] One wonders if Patrick felt reassured at the results of this investigation.

In New York, auxiliaries were increasingly riding with trucks and crews to the scene of fires. On one such occasion, during a blackout, a man was assigned the task of patrolling the fire boxes to guard against false alarms. Before fifteen minutes had elapsed the volunteer was back to the officer in command to report the suspicious presence of "a little guy, about five-foot-two," pacing up and down on the adjoining block. The officer immediately, but with caution, took a few of his men to check out this intelligence. The suspicious character turned out to be the city's mayor.

The peak of membership in the Auxiliary Corps coincided with the first half year of the war when popular fervor for involvement in the overall effort was at its highest. In July of 1942 the auxiliaries numbered 55,410 members. By October of 1943 this had dropped to 32,000, due in large part to the widening of the draft and increase in overtime required in home defense plants. Other members, of course, tired of this time-consuming, often strenuous, volunteer service and simply dropped out.

In the spring of 1944, D-Day and the ensuing Allied victories in Europe made for a rising sense of security that caused volunteers to feel that regular duty was no longer necessary. But London was even then under threat from a new enemy source, submarine-launched robot bombs. In the mayor's estimate it was very premature for New York City to lower its guard and he discussed with Patrick ways to promote new zest within the Corps. One idea they hit upon was the staging of competitive drills among the more than three hundred auxiliary units throughout the city. From these trial performances, five borough champions emerged. Then, on October 14 at City Hall, before the mayor, commissioner and hundreds of spectators, the five best teams demonstrated their skills in handling fire department equipment and their speed in extinguishing mock fires. Even the trained professionals present had to applaud the display. Staten Island took the championship to the disbelief of Brooklyn and The Bronx.

In the effort to keep unit enthusiasm alive, even competitive leagues of softball teams were developed among the auxiliaries. In all, a viable, trained auxiliary force was maintained in readiness until the end of June, 1945, when all civilian protective services were disbanded. The fire department auxiliaries were the final group, the last of the citizen troops to be demobilized.

The auxiliary force had been targeted to lessen shortages of manpower. But scarce equipment soon became a fact of life also, since so many needed items had wartime relatedness. Patrick wrote letter after letter, either himself or through LaGuardia's office, to the Office of Civilian Defense, to the War Production Board, to the Federal Communications Commission, pleading, cajoling, arguing for permission to obtain some commodity.

"Please reconsider your decision to stop the continued manufacture of couplings on the standard gauge," LaGuardia wrote the OCD. Without uniform couplings, New York firemen might go to the assistance of departments in Westchester or Nassau counties and not be able to link their equipment to the water supply there. "This exact condition happened in 1904 in the Baltimore fire, when the present Fire Commissioner of this city was a young engineer on one of the pumpers."[27]

A case had to be made to obtain lead-covered cables for fire-alarm systems. Appeals were even issued for cloth for firemen's uniforms. The official reply was a reminder that fabrics were a priority item for servicemen.

The times called for creative thinking. Walsh reminded the mayor in a memo of May 1, 1942, that, although auxiliary firemen numbered 54,702, the department had not yet received a single piece of auxiliary fire apparatus. "Couldn't we work out a plan with the Sanitation Commissioner that hose reels for cleaning streets be stored overnight in fire company quarters? In the event of a night air raid, we'd have extra reels for fire extinguishment."[28] And an agreement was worked out.

In January of 1943, Commissioner Walsh reported to Mayor LaGuardia that in 1942 the city had seen a decrease of almost six thousand fires over the previous year, all despite the greater hazards brought on by adjustments to the war. Stepped up prevention efforts had been successful. Nevertheless, there was one area where fires had actually increased, an area of deadly danger. Two hundred fires aboard ships had been reported in 1942 as against a hundred and twenty-nine the previous year. Billions of dollars in war materiel were moving hurriedly on overtaxed transport lines through the Port of New York. The waterfront was the fire commissioner's severest challenge.

Every week a committee of key officials met to discuss problems of waterfront safety and defense: representatives of the Army, Navy, Coast Guard, Customs Service, Marine and Aviation, Police and Fire Departments. The Army and Navy were calling on the fire department for guidance in handling hazards such as combustibles and for information on local laws governing the transportation of gasoline and munitions.

No single incident galvanized the city's concern about waterfront hazard as did the burning of the *Normandie*.

In son Michael's household in Brooklyn, a framed photograph was on prominent display in the living room. It showed Patrick Walsh and Mayor LaGuardia standing in conversation on the New York waterfront. Both were dressed in hat and coat against the winter weather and Patrick, at five-foot-six and three-quarters, loomed over the diminutive mayor. What really distinguished the photograph, however, was the huge ship docked at the pier behind the two figures. On its prow was inscribed *Normandie.* Michael's children used to inform their friends that in that photograph Grandpa was telling the Mayor what had to be done to protect the *Normandie* from possible fire. But his advice wasn't followed and the ship burned.

It is as good a story as any. But if Patrick had been aware of the fire hazards aboard the ship that winter he would surely have gotten the mayor to intervene and shut down operations until compliance with city ordinances was met. When conditions were revealed after the disaster, Patrick voiced surprise the fire had not broken out well before February 9, 1942.

The *Normandie,* the biggest ship in the world, accommodated 2,170 passengers. Conceived as a "luxury palace afloat," she had entered New York harbor on her maiden voyage from France in 1935. In August, 1939, she entered New York for the last time. Her French owners, concerned for her safety in the face of spreading war, would not let her sail again.

But when the *Normandie's* host country was drawn into the conflict, the luxury liner became a prime recruit. The Coast Guard took over to convert her into a transport ship for the duration of the war to carry an estimated ten thousand troops on each trans-Atlantic trip. Before the conversion work could get under way, it took 2,400 large moving vans to carry off the *Normandie's* furniture, art deco decorations, elaborate wall murals and huge stock of vintage wines.

The transformation was within a few days of completion. Vast quantities of stores had been temporarily dumped in the lounges and staterooms. Bales of life preservers, in burlap sacks, were stacked in the grand lounge awaiting storage. While workmen in that location were removing by blow torch the lighting stanchions, the last feature of the lounge's luxurious ornamentation, a spark landed on the burlap. "It was like a fire in dry grass," one of the workers later said.

On February 9, the state-of-the-art fire-fighting installations left

The Chief and Mayor LaGuardia make on-the-spot decisions.

on the ship by the French were out of action and the new sprinkler system had not yet been completed. When the NYC Fire Department arrived at the pier the fire was still contained in one area of the ship and there was hope it would be extinguished quickly.

His fear of waterfront fire brought Patrick to the scene twenty minutes after the arrival of the first fire trucks. Smoke shrouded the area around the dock in almost total darkness and on Fifth Avenue, a mile away, the sun was only visible as a dull, red ball. Fire fighters, working from trucks at the pier and fireboats in the water, went full force against the blaze from almost three in the afternoon until six-thirty at night. Tons of water were sent against the fire — Manhattan was at stake as well as the *Normandie*. One author estimates the amount of water at 16,000 tons.[29] The fire was finally under control but the weight of the water she had received made the huge ship list to port. Navy men bored holes in the starboard side hoping to balance her out, but by midnight they issued an "Abandon ship!" order. All persons were evacuated, with a ton of fire equipment remaining behind. In the early hours of the morning, a strong incoming tide caused the *Normandie* to topple to her side and rest in the shallow river bottom.

Two months later, a Naval Court of Inquiry fixed the blame for the fire on the gross carelessness of the workmen. The naval inspector had placed too much reliance on the supervisors of the Robins Dry Dock and Repair Company. However, a separate Senate Naval Affairs Committee attributed the ultimate capsizing of the ship to the undue amount of water placed on board by the fire department. Commissioner Walsh, with the mayor to back him. stood adamant in his contested belief that ninety percent of that water had washed overboard and had not caused the capsizing. In any event, the Senate Naval Committee was not in a position to impose penalties and it does not appear the matter was carried any farther.

The whole *Normandie* episode, occurring as it did at the very outset of America's involvement in the war, greatly increased Patrick's concern about the extreme danger waterfront fires posed to the City of New York. What if a ship carrying explosive munitions had lain close by? It became a personal worry that he could not easily shake off. The real possibility of disaster was always on his mind. In the latter part of 1942 he suffered renewed ulcer attacks and, during a period of four months, was in and out of the Veterans Administration hospital in The Bronx for treatment. Patrick must have been aware of his own vulnerability earlier that year when he sent to the mayor a request for a brief vacation. We know that request was granted because of a letter LaGuardia preserved in his files, the only one of its kind in the dusty archives of his formal correspondence with his fire commissioner. The letter was typed on fire department stationery, Office of the Commissioner, dated May 11, 1942, and reads:

Hon. F.H. LaGuardia
Mayor, City of New York

Dear Sir:

Within my heart is deep recorded
The gift of time by you awarded
By which I hope my nerves to steel
Should dropping bombs around me reel.

Very truly yours,

Patrick Walsh
Fire Commissioner and Chief of Department

That Patrick sent this to the mayor and that LaGuardia thought such humor merited filing reflect the character of the relationship between the two men.

The mayor, of course, was capable of answering in kind. On another occasion when the fire department experienced a close call in a waterfront incident, Commissioner Walsh received an executive document bearing the mayor's signature. It read: "Fire Commissioner is hereby ordered to take exercise on Saturdays by playing golf at nearby golf links. Order to Take Effect Immediately."[30]

On one Saturday when Patrick was obviously obeying the Executive Order with son Joe at Engineers' Golf Club in Roslyn, he was contacted by telephone from headquarters with word that a five-alarm fire was in progress on Amsterdam Avenue in Manhattan. Given the forty-mile drive, Patrick reached the scene in record time. He jumped from the car and trotted toward the firemen, only to be greeted with unrestrained laughter. On his feet were his cleated golf shoes!

CHAPTER TWELVE

Patience and Fortitude

1942 - 1944

"Patience and fortitude," droned the mayor, his quasi-clerical injunction to the listening audience that signed off his Sunday radio program. Only LaGuardia's ebullient personality could have made his weekly "Talk to the People," over WNYC, a media event. New Yorkers tuned in for entertainment at least as much as for information. City commissioners were sure to listen since they never knew when their boss would choose his radio program to issue a direct order to any one of them. Even Robert Moses tuned in.

If there are New Yorkers today who remember LaGuardia's radio performances, most likely they cite the times he read the Sunday morning comics to children during the city's newspaper strike. "Ahhh, what do we have here? The gardener. Stabbed! Bleeding all over the floor.

"Now get this picture. Breathless has hidden herself in a laundry truck . . . along with a pot of money. Fifty . . . thousand . . . dollars. In a pot. Now the truck stops for a traffic light. (You should always stop, children, when the light's red.) Oh, the money — all that money — is spilled out of the pot!"

Even when the subject wasn't the funny papers, LaGuardia entertained. One biographer labeled the radio programs an auditory pastiche which not only revealed what was going on in the world, but also gave advice on what to buy and on how to get rid of cockroaches in the kitchen, as well as notes on blackouts, dollops of morale for those doing volunteer work and comments on food in connections with rationing.[1]

"I do not see many bargains in vegetables this week but I am happy to see that new potatoes are available at five cents a pound; there are also some snap beans that are not very expensive." After meat rationing began, he recommended eating fish so often that New Yorkers started calling him "The Little Flounder."[2]

LaGuardia looked to his commissioners to supply him with material. The fire department dutifully sent over its broadcast bulletins:

> From Patrick Walsh to FHL — Please urge property owners in outlying districts to cut weeds that grow up around fire hydrants and even fire alarm boxes. Citizens should find their way clear to fire alarm boxes for reporting fires in the event of air raids.[3]

One never knew when or how LaGuardia would use material received. On a particular Sunday morning in October, the mayor lectured his audience:

> See to it that rubbish is not accumulating in your halls or in your closets or in the cellar. While on this subject, Pat Walsh said to me, "You just tell your wife you are going to check whether she is using any combustible cleaning fluids." I am sorry, Patty, she is not, and has not been using them for a great many years. If *you* are storing combustible cleaning fluids. . . .[4]

The mayor had already dealt his direct threats to those who stored gasoline in anticipation of rationing. He warned that Commissioner Walsh would have building inspectors confiscate any gasoline found in larger quantity than one gallon because "it could be dangerous as dynamite." Carrying extra fuel on long car trips was also disastrous.[5]

On a late October broadcast, LaGuardia transmitted stern warnings from his fire commissioner against the traditional custom of lighting bonfires on election night. Then on the following Sunday he congratulated his audience since Paddy Walsh had reported both election night bonfires and false alarms had been few in number.

Assistant Chief of Department J.J. McCarthy sent LaGuardia the broadcast suggestion that every motorist carry in his car a two-pound sack of sand for emergency use in the event of fire caused by bombings. Lucky for McCarthy that LaGuardia chose to answer him by mail rather than over the radio:

> Dear John,
>
> We are fighting the Nazis and not the Boy-Scouts. Isn't a two-pound bag a small dose?[6]

The sand idea was set aside the following month when Commissioner Walsh forwarded the mayor a communique to alert citizens to a new German bomb containing a delayed-action devise. The combating tactic now was to apply plenty of water. The use of sand would be dangerous because a person would have to draw too close to the bomb before he could aim sand at it.[7] But sand (no doubt now larger than two-pound doses) was still effective on the traditional incendiary bombs.

New Yorkers responded to LaGuardia's direct radio approach with a flood of letters, some related, others totally unrelated to anything the mayor had said. "If our chief executive is this friendly and informal," went public thinking, "surely he'll lend an interested ear to my request or complaint." The letters, of course, were siphoned off to whichever commissioner might have some connection to the subject.

A Mrs. Bagley in Brooklyn wrote to tell the mayor about her cousin married to a fireman who refused to support his pregnant wife. Mrs. Bagley got her answer:

> . . . Just tell this fireman's wife to take this letter and go and see Commissioner Patrick Walsh of the Fire Department. She will find him a fine, wholesome family man, understanding conditions of this kind, and one who will not countenance such conduct on the part of a member of his department. I am sure he can compel the fireman to provide properly for his wife and expected baby. Just do it this way and I am sure it will have good results.
>
> Very truly yours,
> FHL, Mayor[8]

Some of the letters to the mayor were anonymous and one of these forwarded to Patrick reported that a particular fireman who had been transferred from one engine company to another was planning to kill both his family and himself. Most anonymous letters, less dire than that one, either complained or accused. Tenants on West Sixty-Eighth Street were hanging clothes to dry on fire escapes, a landlord was violating the fire prevention code, such and such a fireman was moonlighting as a bartender in Flatbush.

One letter, duly signed by the citizen, sought consideration of his personal invention of a fire safety device for extinguishing large fires in record time.

Besides the hodgepodge of letters, there were always plenty of other miscellaneous matters that generated communcations between the mayor's office and that of the fire commissioner. From LaGuardia's executive secretary:

> Will you please issue appropriate orders to theFire Department Band so that they will be prepared to play the Yugoslavian National Anthem and ours, when the King of Yugoslavia arrives at Grand Central Terminal July 3rd.[9]

The band might perform for the foreign ruler but restrictions had to be placed on other appearances. According to Commissioner Walsh's memo to the mayor, a reply had been sent to the Catholic chaplain that, owing to the shortage of men, permission would not be granted for the band to play at a Holy Name Rally at Ebbet's Field.[10]

Playing the double role of fire chief and commissioner could have kept Patrick busy day and night. Although as far back as 1927, as assistant chief, he had won the department's Administrative Medal for completely reorganizing the filing and accounting systems of the Bureau of Fire Prevention, it seemed that on the whole organization and administration were not his strong suits. He tended to perform too many tasks himself and not delegate enough assignments to subordinates. The interviewer for the "Profile" in the *New Yorker* drew up a humorous caricature of Patrick Walsh. While other commentators were assessing New York's fire department as the most efficient in the world, the *New Yorker's* breezy description had to contain seeds of truth.

> It is often difficult for Walsh to distinguish between his two offices (Chief and Commissioner). In each role, of course, he gets a good deal of mail and most of this he carries on his person. His clothes have been described as one of the most important filing cabinets in the Department. He has been thinking lately of segregating documents he carries, so that those having to do with the commissionerhood will be in the pockets on his right side and those with his chiefhood on his left, but so far nothing has come of this.[11]

As much as he could feel driven by work, which in the wartime environment never slackened, Patrick still made time for his family. He often talked on the telephone with Mike and Joe. Father Jack was prior at the Dominican House in Louisville, Kentucky, while Father Paul, as member of the Eastern Mission Preaching Band, traveled up and down the coast giving parish missions and retreats. Both dropped in on Patrick whenever they were near New York. If the father could no longer find time for a visit every month to daughter Mary in Lake Ronkonkoma, he did make it on alternate months.

Patrick enjoyed his five grandchildren and took personal interest in them. "Toughen up Frank," he counseled Michael. "You don't want him to fall apart when the army gets hold of him." Catherine hardly cared for the implication that she and her mother had been overprotective of her oldest son. But Michael sided with his father in the opinion that Frank could use the experience of a routine more taxing than his homelife. So, in summer 1941, seventeen and just graduated from St. Augustine's High School, Frank became a hired hand on a Berkshire Hills farm in Sheffield, Massachusetts, while his younger, more fortunate siblings vacationed with Michael, Kitty and Grandma Dundon some fifteen miles away at Twin Lakes, Connecticut. Frank helped to harvest corn and squash, potatoes and tomatoes in a workday that began at sunrise and only ended with the sun's decline. One bright note, he remembers, was that he was expected to operate the farmer's truck and thus got his first driving lessons. Following two years of college and the ROTC at Fordham University, Frank enlisted in the Army Air Corps in May of 1943. Patrick's patriotic fervor scaled new heights now that his own grandson was part of the armed services and ready for action in the World War.

Occasionally, Patrick and Annie invited the family for a Sunday dinner at their Joralemon Street apartment. It was something of a squeeze in the dining room, but Annie goodhumoredly made room for everyone and served a full-course meal out of her tiny kitchen. In the midst of one such afternoon, the superintendent of the building knocked at the door. The neighbors underneath were complaining about the sound of children's feet running back and forth. The Walsh adults had hardly noticed that Kathleen and Patricia had spent the afternoon playing tag from one room to the next.

One such family gathering took place on New Year's Day in 1942. Patrick had started to carve the turkey when the phone rang. A fire was raging practically in his own backyard. Joralemon Street ran down to the Brooklyn harbor and, tied to the pier at the street's end was a burning Brazilian freighter. Michael took over the carving while Patrick made a swift exit.

In covering the few blocks to the dock, Patrick could tell from the strong aroma that the ship's cargo was coffee beans. Conferring with his men on arrival he learned the vessel was in immediate danger of capsizing. Patrick gave an order to train the hoses on the port side ballast tanks. One hundred and twenty-five tons of water were needed to right the ship's keel and dispel any danger of its capsizing. Because of suspicions of sabotage in those early weeks of the war, armed soldiers had arrived to stake out a safety zone around the pier. The fire was declared under control in a few hours and Patrick got back to his apartment before the family left, although he missed the game of Setback.

Holidays, for the most part, were celebrated at Michael's which continued as the natural gathering place for the clan. Mary, Kathleen and Patricia remembered the commotion that always accompanied

Grandpa's arrival with Aunt Annie. Amid the laughter and the loud conversation, each child got a hug and a kiss. Grandpa then moved directly to the piano to sing "Kathleen Mavorneen" to his own accompaniment. Lucky for all it was a brief rendition and exhausted Grandpa's musical repertory. He would swing around on the piano bench smiling and satisfied. Kathleen was always flattered, believing that the song had to be for her alone.

Grandpa loved to memorize poetry — why didn't the girls make a practice of that too? Mary remembers his launching into the recitation of endless verses of a favorite poem while the three granddaughters sat on the carpet at his feet, staring up at him. Mary was bored by the poems but enjoyed the warmer, more loving side of Grandpa that surfaced as he recited.

The children knew that Grandpa had a sterner side, although it was never directed at them. He could sound harsh and angry when telling Mike and Joe about some foolishness committed in his department or by some city bureaucrat he had to deal with. Sometimes he made business-related phone calls during a family gathering and, to the girls, he sounded blunt and impatient. They always felt sorry for whomever was at the other end of the line.

Since Grandpa's attention to the children was usually brief, they knew they had to act fast to hold it. Kathleen remembers calling "Grandpa!" and dropping to the floor to do a somersault across the living-room rug. But Patrick recognized a challenge from whatever source and, before the adults could prevent him, was down on the floor matching Kathleen's feat in a cross-the-room performance. He came up looking gleeful at his accomplishment and the children applauded, but Mike and Catherine were more frightened than impressed.

Patrick never forgot a grandchild's birthday. In the course of the afternoon, a black-chauffeured car pulled up in front of 1193 East 19th Street and the driver delivered a birthday greeting to the eager child. Inside the card was always a new twenty-dollar bill, a marvelous present to a youngster in the early 1940's.

The children were always immensely proud to have a grandfather who was Fire Commissioner of New York City. Kathleen remembers sitting at the Saturday matinee at the Elm movie theater on Avenue M and thrilling when the words flashed on the screen, "No smoking by order of Fire Commissioner Patrick Walsh." She would elbow her friend in the adjoining seat, "That's my grandfather — pass it along!"

But Kathleen never hesitated to join school friends on the mile walk home as they collected used Christmas trees discarded along the curbs. Piling them high in a vacant lot, she thought it terribly exciting to see how one match could send giant, crackling flames leaping toward the sky. When Catherine found out, considerations of safety were not foremost in her mind. "What would your grandfather say!" she screamed. Catherine still found her father-in-law formidable in that he was not slow to scold the adults if he thought it warranted.

The children were included in yearly fire department outings to Steeplechase and got front-row tickets to the Fire-Police Departments' baseball games in Yankee Stadium. Not only the grandchildren were invited but also nieces and nephews of daughters-in-law Betty and Mary Bergen. One of these nephews recalled his fright at Patrick's gruff manner. The chief piled them all into his shining, red fire car with, "Come on, boys, can't you keep moving?" But by afternoon's end the chief seemed much kinder, having insured that each child received whatever treat he or she wanted.

Patrick took particular pride in the career and accomplishments of his eldest son. Michael's term as New York Secretary of State ended with Governor Lehman's retirement from office at the close of 1942. On that November's ballot, Michael's name was entered for State Supreme Court Judge by both Democratic and Republican parties, thus assuring his election. After the swearing-in, in January, 1943, Patrick sat at Michael's side at the banquet in Brooklyn's Hotel Bossert.

An official photograph of that luncheon survives, thirty-six people seated around a horseshoe table in a private dining room. Among the nine priests present in their Roman collars was Father Joseph

166/ LaGuardia's Fire Chief

Steadman, author of a popular daily missal and close friend and classmate of Michael's. Patrick Scanlon, the controversial editor of the Brooklyn *Tablet* was also a guest. Both Patrick and Michael knew and admired him, supporting the newspaper's conservative Catholic viewpoint prevalent at the time.

Addressing some remarks to the clergy, judges and friends at the banquet, Michael expressed gratitude to those people who had made the day possible, "starting with my esteemed father, still my chief guide, though he has cautioned me never again to eulogize him in public."

The following year held what was perhaps an even prouder moment for Patrick when Michael was named Knight of St. Gregory, a papal honor bestowed on selected laymen recommended by their bishops for having rendered special services in their dioceses. On the day of his solemn enrollment in the Order of St. Gregory, five knights, replete with sword and sash, shared the honor of the occasion. At the end of the ceremony, each had the chance to give a brief acknowledgement and Michael began his with a proud observation: "I am the only honoree today who has his father present to witness the moment."

But as much as Michael and his family were gratifying to Patrick, the three daughters-in-law always felt the father favored and admired the religious members of the family above his married sons. That most Irish of convictions was probably at play, namely that priestly sons are God's supreme give to parents. Catherine was resentful that any money gifts inevitably went to the Dominicans or to the Cenacle, the parish or the diocese. Although Michael had a salary of a judge, rearing five children through college, coupled with social and charitable obligations that accompanied his public positions, brought him constant financial headaches. Catherine always thought her father-in-law might have helped out a bit, but Patrick probably never perceived any problem and Michael would have been the last person to mention it.

Patrick had never focused on the psychological development of his children. He was not one to ask about feelings or observe the subtle reactions. Rather, the children were oriented to their father's reactions and expectations and were always striving to measure up to the standards he held out to them. Michael measured up perfectly, even in the matter of agreeing with his father that the religious in the family were the most deserving of gifts.

CHAPTER THIRTEEN

A Fire Department Civil War

1943 - 1944

Once a full-scale military draft was in effect, the tug-of-war started between the Army and the homefront over available manpower. During the early years of the draft, LaGuardia made every effort to obtain military deferments for the city police and firemen. Former Commissioner McElligott had appealed to the draft boards for exemptions as early as 1940. During the mayor's speech at the 1941 presentation of medals to the fire and police departments, he paid his "respects" to the "fatheads" of the Selective Service Administration who opposed his bid for draft exemptions.

Once the blitz had begun in England, all firemen and policemen in the armed forces were sent home, their services considered essential to the protection of life and property under the constant threat of bomb-related fires. Now New York could become a target of attack and fire department staffing had to be at full complement to guarantee preparedness. Some local draft boards were deferring firemen while others were not.

In the "Commissioner's Message" prefacing the fire department's Annual Report published some months before Pearl Harbor, Patrick wrote:

> It may not be, as a rule, proper to discuss controversial matters in a foreword such as this. But for the record I must reiterate my position regarding the conscription of firemen under the Selective Service Act. It is not that I in any way question the wisdom of that act or that I seek special privileges for members of the uniformed force. From the start it seemed to me obvious that men specially trained in fire extinguishment, belonging to a

semi-military organization, accustomed to discipline themselves and understanding the use of authority, should not be sent to training camps. . . . The arguments have been presented at great length and His Honor, the Mayor, has protested to the highest authorities against this conscription.

With the outbreak of war, some firemen were caught up in the surge of patriotism that swept the country and resigned their jobs to enlist in the services. This was very upsetting to Patrick. His task was to convince his men the vehicle for their patriotism was their home fire department. One issue of the firemen's magazine *WNYF* featured on its cover, in heroic posture, fire fighters enlisted as soldiers, sailors and marines.[1] It was the kind of propaganda Patrick hoped to deflect.

While discouraging enlistments among young firemen, the commissioner also had to confront slippage at the other end — early retirement available after twenty years of service. "Think seriously before submitting applications for retirement," Patrick lectured. "Avoid committing a public disservice in exchange for a few paltry dollars and a life of ease." And the preacher in him added, "We come into the world without anything and we leave it similarly."[2] These remarks reminded some of his friends that the department had attempted three years earlier to lure older members of the department into retirement with increased pensions as bait. Patrick, as an older member, had spurned the offer, saying that when he went to bed at night, he liked "to sleep the sleep of the just."[3]

By 1943, as the war deepened with no end in sight, manpower had become an increasingly scarce resource and the city administration's struggle with the Selective Service intensified. But Selective Service had the muscle and would continue to include firemen in the draft, leaving the city to innovate as best it could.

By July, Walsh estimated that the department was short 1,200 men. Six hundred of these were in the military services and another significant number represented continuing retirements. "You can't stop them," Patrick observed wearily. The *New York Times* noted,

"Fire officials close to the Commissioner expressed anxiety for the safety of the city in the event of a large fire in view of the shortage of manpower of which Mr. Walsh spoke."[4] The Auxiliary Corps was essentially a reserve to be used in the event of a major disaster and could not substitute for the regular service of trained firemen.

When questioned earlier in the year as to whether the fire department might have to counteract shortages of manpower by abandoning the eight-hour day (the three-platoon system), Walsh had replied, "There is no thought of any such change."[5] But by the end of 1943 there was not only the thought but the implementation. On December 30, the commissioner issued Special Order No. 258 imposing on all department members three additional eight-hour tours of duty in every twenty-day cycle. "I don't care what system we use," said Walsh, "as long as we have enough men."[6]

"Illegal," "Mandatory overtime," responded the Uniformed Firemen's Association. "A violation of the three-platoon law," accused Vincent Kane, UFA President.

Kane, the association's talented leader, nearly six feet tall and weighing two hundred and fifty pounds, had been active in the firemen's union since the early 1920's. In 1930 he was counted among the young Turks who displaced the "old guard" leadership and Kane was elected union president, a post he retained until 1945. His drive was toward strengthening the firemen's association by affiliating it with the larger labor movement represented by the American Federation of Labor. With the personal skill of an experienced labor leader, he had brought his organization's disputing factions into a working harmony and had steadily built up its power and prestige.

The relationship between Patrick Walsh and the Uniformed Firemen's Association had started out on the best of terms. When Patrick was appointed commissioner, the UFA had given him a testimonial luncheon attended by two thousand members. Shortly after this, on the occasion of a dinner marking the opening of a Fire Department American Legion Post, Vincent Kane said in a speech that Commissioner Walsh ". . . has rejuvenated this department in less than a month. He's a square-shooter, on the level, and I'm here to tell you, and I don't care how far my voice reaches, that there is new joy in this Fire Department. . . ."[7] Kane had been most sincere in his remarks, but circumstances a few years later had deeply altered that climate of good will.

On December 31, eighteen hundred UFA members met for five hours behind closed doors. The press was barred but participants described the meeting as "quite stormy" and reported that LaGuardia's name was booed.

The UFA was legally barred from striking but pledged to challenge the fire commissioner's decree in court. It immediately sought a "show cause" order accusing Patrick Walsh of having made a "deliberate and unlawful attempt to destroy the three-platoon system as provided for in the Administrative Code of the City of New York." The matter would go to trial the following month.

Vincent Kane's Uniformed Firemen's Association had a membership of 6,590 men in January, 1944. The officer ranks of the fire department were organized separately in three levels of associations (lieutenants, captains, chiefs), with a joint total of under two thousand men. The officers' associations, however, agreed to accept the mayor's proposal.

LaGuardia took a stronger measure. Canceling the automatic payment of an annual cost-of-living bonus of four hundred and twenty dollars per fireman, he now announced the bonus would be paid only in exchange for the individual fireman's commitment to the extra-duty decree. The union's rejection of the bonus in lieu of straight overtime pay was not a purely financial issue. The bonus represented a dollar and three cents as compared to the regular dollar and fourteen cents a fireman would have earned for the extra hours worked. But a bonus did not add to one's pension account as straight time payment would. More than the dollars and cents issue, however, was the men's resentment of the basic proposal that overtime should be forced on them and the payment termed euphemistically a "bonus."

In late January, 1944, the International Association of Fire Chiefs held its annual meeting in New York and the mayor and Patrick were present as hosts. LaGuardia never lost an opportunity for press coverage, especially if he were promoting some divisive issue. Without pause to question whether the association had any particular interest in the civil war within the host fire department, LaGuardia sailed into the topic and sermonized his listeners. During the war, you could not talk of overtime in the fire department any more than you could talk of overtime in the Army, he maintained. The same discipline had to prevail in the one service as in the other.[8]

The UFA's suit was brought to trial in state court February 21, before Justice Louis A. Valente. It was, from the outset, a recognized fact that, in certain situations, the eight-hour shift or three-platoon system could be suspended. However, the law limited these circumstances to "conflagrations, riots or other similar emergencies." The interpretation of the word "emergency" became the core issue of the trial.

Union spokesman Kane reasoned that no true emergency existed. There was only a manpower shortage in the fire department, he declared, because the commissioner had not made sufficient appointments from the list of eligible applicants.

On the last day of February Patrick took the stand. He countermanded Kane's argument by pointing to the futility of appointing new firemen who would be immediately eligible for the draft and he cited numerous appeals to national and local directors of the Selective Service Administration for the exemption of all uniformed city firemen.

By the end of 1943, however, Walsh and LaGuardia had given up their fruitless appeals to the draft boards. The prolongation of the war was forcing recruiters to scratch the bottom of the manpower barrel. When fathers of families became subject to the draft, it also became harder to discourage single firemen from enlisting or to continue a campaign to obtain blanket exemptions for them. The only alternative the mayor and his commissioner felt remained to them was to impose extra duty on the depleted numbers of the firemen ranks.

The trial's verdict was handed down in a month's time. The

March 25 edition of the *New York Times* announced, "Extra Duty Upheld for City's Firemen." "Justice Valente Dismisses Suit to Restrain Walsh from Enforcing the Decree. Emergency Said To Exist." In the judge's words:

> The embarkation of troops, the storage and transportation of munitions, explosives, volatile inflammable liquids and combustibles, the equipping and refitting of ships, the conduct of war industries, all have a tendency to considerably increase fire hazards.

As far back as September, 1939, President Roosevelt had declared the existence of a national emergency. Certainly the years of war had increased it, and New York City shared that emergency.

The two-platoon system went into effect when, on May 1, a twelve-hour day was mandated for three hundred firemen and fifty-five officers assigned to Staten Island's twenty-three companies. On May 26 it was extended to selected areas of Brooklyn and Queens. Coney Island and the Rockaways were included so that firehouse staffing would be at full complement during the busy summer season. One thousand additional firemen were now on the twelve-hour day.

The war over extra duty was being waged in the newspapers as well as in the courts. Patrick had always prided himself on the unity he promoted within the force. Now the dissension that had erupted was spread out for all to see. The situation must have hurt him deeply.

It was bad enough that the union was warring with him in the press. But for an individual fireman to make a public criticism of his department went beyond all tolerable bounds. Further, it violated department regulations and required immediate punishment. John P. Crane, a fireman first grade, distributed a letter to the newspapers claiming that the reintroduction of the two-platoon system was "unnecessary" and he accused the mayor of "persecuting" firemen by refusing them the cost of living bonus.

Discipline quickly followed. Crane was transferred from his

firehouse in The Bronx to one in Stapleton, Staten Island. He now had to travel two to three hours a day in addition to his twelve-hour shift.

But John Crane was not a lonely voice; he was vice-president of the union. His supporters claimed his statements to the press had been delivered in that capacity and that he had not violated department rules. When five members of the Lieutenants' Association issued a statement accusing Commissioner Walsh of branding firemen joining the armed forces as "slackers" and "unpatriotic" because they were abandoning the city in an emergency, these five were also transferred to posts at some distance from their homes. Mayor LaGuardia, when questioned about the transfers, claimed he was not familiar with the details. "I refer all questions to Commissioner Walsh who is my source on fire matters."[9]

The transfers caused an uproar. The City Council adopted a resolution criticizing the mayor and fire commissioner. Walter Winchell, in his June 4 radio broadcast, declared: "This is to inform Fire Commissioner Walsh that he is hired to run the NYC Fire Department and not a Berlin Gestapo or a private Siberia. Criticizing Mayor LaGuardia is not a crime. It is a constitutional right and all city employees are American citizens."[10]

The *Civil Service Leader* claimed that ". . . the Commissioner of the New York Fire Department is involved in one of the most spectacular battles in civil service history — against his own men. He has put the gag upon spokesmen of two employee organizations in his department. . . ."[11]

In a letter to the commissioner, the American Civil Liberties Union requested a reconsideration of the "whole policy of transferring men for exercising their rights of free speech, particularly where they are acting as authorized officials of recognized unions of departmental employees."[12]

Walsh, meanwhile, challenged any city fireman to show him how the city could properly be protected at this juncture of the war without resorting to extra tours of duty. He would award that individual the department's Administrative Medal. Sheer necessity, and no other consideration, he maintained, had made him take the unpopular measure.

> At my time of life, with over forty years in the Fire Department, I am not concerned with any political aspirations. When I leave the Fire Department it will not be for another position. I speak without personal prejudice and without personal ambitions when I say that I regret the two-platoon system has had to be installed in certain districts and will have to be extended. I know that when the manpower shortage in this country is eased, the three-platoon system will return.[13]

A response soon came from five lieutenants who publicly retracted that part of their statement which had accused the commissioner of branding as "slackers" all firemen who quit the department to enter the armed forces. According to the *New York Times,* Commissioner Walsh, when informed of the retraction, declared, "I am well satisfied. I am not vindictive and never have been. I naturally did not want to be accused of saying something I never did or would say. I had two sons in the last war. My brother was killed in that war and my grandson is serving in the Air Corps in the present war. The transfers will be readjusted soon. The incident is now closed."[14]

The status of Fireman Crane, however, remained unchanged. No retraction had been received from him and he was still commuting from The Bronx to his post on Staten Island. It would be almost a year before his return to Manhattan and within a month he filed a futile suit in State Supreme Court for payment of the overtime he was forced to work. But his efforts were rewarded in another sense. In April, 1945, he unseated Vincent Kane and was elected president of the Uniformed Firemen's Association.

The end of the overtime battle was in sight. The union's court appeal had not succeeded and the Appellate Division denied their right to bring their case to the State Court of Appeals. There was nowhere else to go.

Spokesmen for the New York State Federation of Labor, umbrella organization for the UFA, now urged city firemen to sign the waivers. On June 29, the UFA itself finally bowed, adopting a resolution advising its members to go along with this prerequisite for receiving their bonuses. At the mayor's request, the City Board of Estimate voted unanimously to earmark three million dollars in the 1944-1945 budget for the fire department cost-of-living bonuses.

By July 4, 1944, Commissioner Walsh reported that ninety-nine percent of the department had signed waivers and said he was "very proud" of his men's cooperation.[15] The troops had surrendered and the revolt was over.

But the air was never cleared. "The big source of trouble is this," a columnist had written in a January issue of the *Civil Service Leader*, "men don't trust the mayor or Fire Commissioner Walsh."[16] Had the commissioner truly done everything possible to obtain draft deferments, adopting the overtime measure only as a last resort? The case was pleaded on both sides but repeated court decisions could not resolve feelings at the grassroots level.When Mayor LaGuardia had appointed Patrick commissioner in 1941, one department columnist had written that the firemen themselves would have elected Walsh to the position had they been given the chance to vote.[17] As assistant chief in 1936, he had been described as the most beloved man in the fire department. Where had the popularity come from and how did Patrick carry his leadership?

At Patrick's appointment, local commentators on fire department happenings made a host of observations — "McElligott was never close to his men while Patrick Walsh is — Walsh carried the nickname 'Smily Pat' during thirty-nine years in the department — a humane and understanding administration is now in charge of the 11th Floor (Municipal Building)."[18] He could be stern and exact discipline, but Patrick had also projected a quality of personal interest and concern that his men had perceived as genuine. The sincerity of this Christmas message was never questioned:

> . . . I would like very much to be able to greet you, one and all, and wish you well. . . . My wealth is my host of friends and comrades, the men I have known and worked with and the

thousands of men with whom, though our contact has been brief or official, carry the insignia of the Fire Department in their hearts as well as on their caps . . . . In them I reavow my faith and trust and pride. To them I extend my gratitude for splendid cooperation and loyalty.[19]

Patrick's characteristic response to any commendation was, "I could do nothing without my men." He probably thought of himself, first and foremost, as the father of a big family. When he read in the newspaper one summer's day that a New York City fireman had won a national rowing competition on the Schuylkill River in Philadelphia, he was "all aglow. The Commissioner was as happy over the result in Philadelphia as though it were the fire department that had won the event and not the Ravenswood Rowing Club."[20]

But, just as in his own smaller family, the loving father held all the authority. He assumed his men understood they "belonged to a semi-military organization, accustomed to discipline . . . and understanding the use of authority."[21] Conformity was expected. The fire department, much like the Army with which Patrick readily compared it, had entrenched traditions and modes of operation which were to be respected, not questioned. As a commissioner who had risen through the uniformed service, Patrick was very familiar with these traditions and felt it his duty to embody them. "Set the example and your men will follow suit," was the advice he loved to give his officers.

On one occasion Patrick provoked criticism by an unanticipated promotion of men to deputy chief positions just before the civil service list expired. The *New York Times* printed his forthright explanation:

I made these appointments from the names left on the present list because I wanted to avail myself of the services of these experienced men as Deputy Chiefs. . . . Since the three-platoon system was established (1936), this has been a young department from the standpoint of length of service. I did not want to wait for a new list because the men passing examinations and getting places on that list would probably be pretty young in point of service and we need old-time firemen, with old-time experience.[22]

And the old-time fireman prided himself on a filial loyalty to his superiors. In Patrick's estimation, Mayor LaGuardia could not have offered him higher praise than by calling him "a great source of help and comfort to me. . . . No problem has been too difficult to be cheerfully undertaken and beautifully performed."[23]

But the times were changing and younger men entering the fire department had different views. They were better educated and from socio-economic backgrounds that had vastly improved since the turn of the century. They were more willing to question authority than their fathers had been and the introduction of unions into the city's uniformed forces was a vehicle for doing this. Much as Patrick took pains to be helpful when confronted with the problems of an individual fireman, it was another case entirely when an individual considered it his right to set before the commissioner a grievance against the system. Wrote one critic of the traditional approach:

In 1945 regular meetings of the representatives of officers and firemen with the First Deputy Commissioner were announced by Fire Commissioner Walsh, but the next month the plan was abandoned. The deeply established autocracy in these departments (fire and police) will defeat any type of consultation which is not compelled by law. . . .[24]

Some of the great difficulty Patrick experienced with the overtime issue from 1943 to 1945 could have been reduced had he been better able to accept the idea of his men bargaining for their perceived rights through the medium of unions.

How much trust and support Patrick lost during the long course of the overtime battle cannot be measured. He never let surface within the department his personal hurt at the loss of his men's esteem. His bare allusion to the happenings in his magazine editorial of January, 1946, was as impersonal as it was generous to his men.

"Internal problems in the department never affected the men's performance as firefighters," it said.[25]

Four years earlier Patrick had quoted lines which current circumstances had made particularly appropriate:

"And if you shrug away the advice of older, experienced men, reflect as I did on

Fools of the jest, whom God flays ever and again
We, who thought old men odd, are now the odd old men."[26]

CHAPTER FOURTEEN

Winding Down

1945 - 1946

An enemy confronted the fire department in the early winter of 1945: the weather. That January set record lows for New York City. The average temperature for the first thirty-five days of the year was seventeen degrees and on no single day did the mercury reach thirty-two. Snow and ice accumulated in the harbor making traffic conditions hazardous and tying up shipping facilities essential to the war effort.

Fire alarms were turned in in record numbers as overworked heating systems broke down, leading people to experiment dangerously with alternate means of keeping warm. Seven fire fighters lost their lives between January 1 and February 16. On January 27, Patrick shuttled between two multiple alarm fires, a four-story warehouse for paper stock in Red Hook and a five-story factory in Williamsburg. In Red Hook, Battalion Chief Anthony Jireck collapsed from heat and smoke and subsequently died. Patrick had known him well. They had fought that South Brooklyn warehouse fire together in 1936, were trapped, and managed to escape via the roof at the last minute.

Patrick always said the fireman's greatest triumph was saving lives and his severest trial was witnessing the suffering and death brought on by fire. His son Paul remembered from the early days that the smell of burning bodies haunted Patrick for weeks. The death of a brother fireman was always a personal sorrow and particularly that of a veteran like Jireck whom he had known and worked with. As head of department, Patrick felt responsible for the lives of his men. The overtime struggle of 1944 had aged the commissioner and the seven firemen deaths in early 1945 intensified that process. Although it was winter that took the toll on firemen's lives, the most dramatic fire of that year occurred during the heat of the following summer. The scene was the Empire State Building on July 28, 1945. At ten a.m. on a warm Saturday, an Army B-25 two-engine bomber approached New York City and was advised by controls, in the midst of a blinding fog, to land at LaGuardia Airport. For reasons unknown, the pilot decided to head for Newark. Although aircraft were required to maintain a two thousand-foot altitude over Manhattan, the B-25 was cruising at nine hundred and thirteen feet above the ground. Its impact with the 1,258-foot Empire State Building was at the seventy-eighth and seventy-ninth floors, tearing a hole in the north wall eighteen by twenty feet wide. Eleven employees working in the seventy-ninth-floor offices of the National Catholic Welfare Conference were killed instantly, as were the plane's three crewmen.

At the tremendous collision, flaming gasoline sprayed over a ten-story radius and set aflame the cans of paint in storage on the seventy-eighth floor. One portion of the plane crashed through the elevator-shaft wall, plummeting to the pit below street level and bursting into flames. Other portions dropped on an adjoining building, setting that on fire also. One piece of debris sailed for five blocks and damaged a building at Fifth Avenue and Twenty-Ninth Street.

Fire safety technology in the construction of skyscrapers had taken a quantum leap by 1945 and the fire-resistant construction materials in the Empire State, as well as the giant structure's built-in sprinkler system, contained the flames, preventing their spreading beyond the immediate ten floors.

Patrick took personal command of the twenty-three fire companies and forty-one pieces of equipment that quickly arrived at the scene. Firemen squeezed hoses and portable apparatus into the elevators that were still operating to the sixtieth floor. None could function above that, so the men were forced to lug their equipment up eighteen flights of stairs to the source of the fire on the seventy-eighth floor. Having panted up the last flight, they were immensely relieved to discover the building's eight-inch standpipes were undamaged by the blast and ample water pressure was still available. All flames were extinguished in forty minutes.[1]

Although fourteen lives had been lost, Patrick thanked the Almighty that at least the collision had occurred on a weekend. Had it been a week day, hundreds of people would have been working on the ten floors affected by the crash. Patrick remarked to the press that, although it was the first fire at such a high altitude, it had been comparatively easy to extinguish.

Victory in Europe in the spring of 1945 heightened people's hopes for a final end to the war. As guest speaker at the fire department's Holy Name Society Communion Breakfast in April, Patrick promised the thousand firemen present that the end of the war emergency would restore normal working hours. It would also "give me the chance to get out." He told them he had remained at his post because "the department has been good to me. I am blessed with good health and I feel it is my duty to work during the war."[2]

With victory on the Japanese front in August, expectations were high for quick return to the three-platoon system. The commissioner promised it would be restored as soon as it was "mathematically possible" to do so. Only 5,561 men were currently on the rolls, with retirements being filed at a rate of twenty-three per month. Only a trickle of men had returned from the armed services and the resumption of the three-platoon system would require at least 8,647 on active duty.[3] Actually, it was a year later and a subsequent commissioner who judged conditions ready for the transition back to an eight-hour day.

Although a general relief prevailed at war's end, Patrick emphasized the continuing need for safety precautions against fires. As the military forces withdrew their personnel assigned to local fire inspections, a vacuum would be left. In his WNYF editorial of October, 1945, he counseled manufacturers and businessmen who had dealt with war contracts to enact their own rigid fire-prevention measures as they converted to peacetime production. He drew attention to the fact that six million new homes were on the drawing boards for 1946 and builders should consider fireproofing procedures as "musts."

With the war finally over, Patrick knew he was in the closing months of his career. The fact he had reached his seventy-seventh birthday and was exhausted from the responsibilities of his position in a wartime environment might not have been the overriding reason for his retirement. Key to his decision was the mayor's announcement he would not seek a fourth term. LaGuardia had let it be known that, although he had full confidence in his ability to win another election, it was his opinion the office should not be held too long by one individual. And besides, he conceded in partial jest, people might be getting a little tired of him.

An important factor in LaGuardia's decision not to run again was President Roosevelt's death in April, 1945. With the passing of his long-time friend and supporter, the mayor could not expect from the Truman Administration the essential federal monies he had obtained through Roosevelt. LaGuardia's physical condition was also a consideration since his health had deteriorated with the strenuous pace of twelve years in the mayor's office. Finally, LaGuardia had had word that the Republican party would not back his renomination. And even this irrepressible politician could no longer relish the prospect of regrouping himself for yet another all-out battle. Instead, he would wave good-bye to City Hall with head held high.[4]

Patrick was reluctant to see him go. When the postmaster of Union City, New Jersey, asked if he could have LaGuardia's fire helmet, since the postmaster occasionally investigated fires in letter boxes, Patrick replied:

> Mayor LaGuardia will still be an honorary member of the New York Fire Department. The helmet will certainly be kept by him and, since he will remain an honorary member, we expect that he will attend all large fires.[5]

The mayor's cabinet would be leaving with him, and on November 18, LaGuardia formally made an announcement of the retirements, to become effective the last day of the year. The *New York Times* recorded his mention of each departing official.

For Fire Commissioner Walsh, the Mayor reserved special and personal commendation. He was "a great fireman, extremely devoted to the department," the Mayor declared.[6]

When LaGuardia gave his final Sunday's "Talk to the People," Patrick stood around at the radio station with other solemn-looking members of the administration.

On New Year's Day, 1946, the retired mayor ritualistically led his successor, William O'Dwyer, into City Hall and turned over to him the city government. "Before stepping into his wife's car, LaGuardia turned, took off the big, black hat that had become his trademark and, smiling broadly, waved to City Hall and said good-bye."[7]

An editor of the *New York Times* later tried to encapsulate the twelve years of LaGuardia's colorful leadership:

He did not find us brick and leave us marble, but he rescued our public credit, put non-partisan experts in charge of city departments, expanded parks and playgrounds, developed clinics, public markets, housing projects, airports. He did much of this in an uproar of controversy, but he did it.[8]

As much as Patrick's work was his life and the demands of his career renewed his energies as well as depleted them, one side of the man had genuinely looked forward to retirement. He would get to read so many books he never had time for. He would deepen his study of theology and make weekend retreats to renew his prayer life. And he would write. The autobiography begun two years earlier was just one chapter long. He had left off with himself still a boy in Ireland making the decision to sail for America. He certainly wanted to continue it. Maybe he would even try to write more poetry.

And there would now be more time for his family, golf with Mike and Joe, perhaps short trips to visit Jack and Paul at their different posts and, of course, Mary Florence in Ronkonkoma. Grandson Frank had come home safely from Saipan in the Pacific and was finishing college at Fordham University in preparation for Columbia Law School. Young Jack was in his freshman year at Holy Cross College. Patrick would be seeing more of the grandchildren. But, during the first months of 1946, the man seemed listless. He was tired and it was winter. Certainly, the family thought, he would feel himself again by spring. But the mental energy did not seem to pick up. The books went unread, the autobiography untouched. His sons were deeply concerned.

One development that may have depressed Patrick's spirits during this time was an action taken by his successor, Frank Quayle, the fire commissioner appointed by the new Mayor O'Dwyer. In contrast to Patrick who had come up through the fire department ranks, Quayle was a former business executive and Brooklyn postmaster, brought into the top fire department post as an administrator. Only a few months into his new responsibilities, Quayle appointed a committee to survey the entire department, with a view to studying the feasibility of closing some fire houses and opening others, reorganizing personnel and equipment to increase overall efficiency and effectiveness.

The new administration based its survey initiative on the fact no wholesale reorganization of the fire department had taken place since the turn of the century. New fire houses had been opened as the city grew but none had been closed or transferred from areas where they were no longer needed. This part of the survey hardly reflected on Patrick's performance. His many predecessors had not taken on the job of reorganization and Patrick could hardly have done so even had he been convinced of its necessity. His mandate was to respond to the pervasive demands of fire department operations in wartime and any other agendas had to be held in abeyance.

But the Quayle report criticized a management style which, though not originating with Patrick, certainly continued during his term. The report dealt with specifics that had to reflect on the chief administrator who had stepped down just four months earlier. Reference was made to an overly monolithic organization resistant to change and the adoption of new techniques. The absence of overall planning was cited as well as failure to make effective use of the many statistical reports the department generated. The criticisms were really directed against the fire department of the prior half century, but Patrick was the only one still around to embody those times.

Although the nature of the survey was construed to be highly confidential, most likely Patrick, with his contacts throughout the department, was well aware it was under way. Knowledge of it must have worried him, hurt him and left him feeling somewhat betrayed. He had given his life's blood to directing New York's fire department during wartime, but both he and the record of his service seemed unappreciated.

What also hurt Patrick was the experience he shared with countless other public officials and administrators on the day after their terms ended. They discovered they were expendable. Once Patrick stepped aside, he was out of the picture.

Although available for consultation, no one from the fire department asked him a question or sought to tap the expertise of his forty-five years of service. What made the situation harder to accept for Patrick was that both Mayor O'Dwyer and Commissioner Quayle were Irish. "How could they treat their own so poorly?" was how he seemed to regard what had happened.

To direct his father's attention from these concerns, Joe suggested he plan a trip to Ireland. Almost twenty years had gone by since Patrick had returned there with Mary Ann and found so much pleasure in seeing relatives and revisiting scenes of his childhood. Annie would accompany him and Jack and Paul arranged to go along for the first few weeks. The four left on a Pan American Clipper on June 18, 1946.

The relatives in Tipperary were delighted to welcome the native son turned fire commissioner of New York City, and his sister Alice still lived on the original family farm in Ballydine. At times Patrick responded in his normal, enthusiastic manner, even dancing a jig at a party given in his honor. But at other times his mind seemed to wander and he gave the appearance of being only partially present to the people around him. A limp he had developed became more noticeable. Paul remembered his father commenting to him that Ireland had changed, that the grass was not so green as before and the birds no longer sang so loud.

Patrick and Annie remained in Ireland a full two months and Patrick seemed to gradually relax into the pace of rural Tipperary. But on the plane trip home a frightening episode occurred. Patrick suddenly felt weak and began to disassociate himself from his surroundings. In his ensuing agitation and confusion, he made an attempt to find an exit and several flight attendants were needed to restrain him. The crew wired ahead and the fire department's physician was at the airport when the plane landed.

Patrick was hospitalized immediately at the West Hill Sanitarium in The Bronx. It was August 25. Although he rallied periodically during the following weeks, his overall condition was steadily weakening and he finally suffered a major stroke. Annie and one or other of the sons were with him constantly and watched him slip into a coma. While Father Paul, who had given him the last rites, held his hand, Patrick died in the early morning of September 21, 1946.

CHAPTER FIFTEEN

Summing Up a Life
1868 - 1946

 When Patrick Walsh sat down in the 1940's to write what he intended to be an autobiography, he sought to justify such an undertaking to himself and to his family. He confessed he harbored "no delusive thought that the world will ever note, or even be remotely interested in what I have to say." But he had personal reasons for chronicling the memories of his lifetime.

The death of several of his friends had increased Patrick's reflections on his own mortality. Already in his middle seventies, he felt an urge to examine the happenings of his life and draw out their meaning. Apologizing for such digressions from the busy, real world of a fire chief and commissioner, he made a point of emphasizing in his stylized prose, "I never tarry too long in these reminiscent interludes and always return from them to the humdrum of routine matters with a freshened spirit and an avidity for action that is gratifying."

His second purpose was to instruct succeeding generations by leaving to his family the record of a way of life:

> May these words provide some small heritage, some consoling testimonial to those grand and ever loving children who have furnished me with so much personal satisfaction. May it offer in turn to their children a picture, however incomplete, that provides at least a general outline of a common ancestor and a pattern ofthe way of life in which their parents were reared.

A way of life. The implication is that of conscious choice of a particular direction to follow. For Patrick, it is safe to say the total embodiment of his chosen way could be found in his religion. He firmly believed Catholicism provided all he needed to know to lead a good and moral life and the guidance he required for the choices and decisions of his everyday existence.

In a discarded draft of the introduction to his autobiography, Patrick had written in his large, rather awkward penmanship: "It is not very many years ago since reading in one of Father Gillis' books,

> Vast libraries of pretentious books have been written in an attempt to expound what men call a philosophy of life. But there is no philosophy of life so sublime as that which comes out of the mouths of babies when they begin to prattle the words of the catechism, God made me to know Him, to love Him and serve Him in this life and to be happy with Him forever in the next.

"Yes," added Patrick, "that philosophy has been ever mine." And to Patrick these words went beyond philosophy to inspire his personal faith. One granddaughter remembered attending the three-hour Good Friday devotions with Patrick at St. Charles church. She was impressed by the way he knelt straight up for long periods in an attitude of great reverence.

Although the Bible's New Testament teaches that the greatest of the virtues is charity, the Irish Catholic seemed prone to give at least equal status to obedience. The voice of authority was clear and unmistakable, centered primarily in the church and, by derivation, in family and government. Every question had a right and wrong, with small margin for the nebulous gray area. In relation to both church and country, Patrick was the humble son. In his family, he was the voice of authority. His daughter-in-law Catherine claimed that Patrick could control his sons with one look.

But other aspects of Patrick's personality softened the picture of the authoritarian and the strict disciplinarian: his genuine concern for people, his sense of humor and his personal simplicity.

Patrick always gave credit to his men for the department's accomplishments. Time and again he emphasized that he could do nothing without them. His men knew that such statements from the commissioner were not empty phrases. Ever since his days as captain of Engine Company 7 on Duane Street, Patrick was known by his subordinates for his readiness to submit descriptions of their bravery for department awards while omitting the examples of his own heroics.

His sincerity and concern for his men showed in other ways also. It was common knowledge that Walsh would look hard for ways to circumvent the dismissal of a fireman. Not only did he feel for the individual involved but he was concerned about the welfare of the wife and children. He would find the time to counsel the man personally in an effort to resolve the problem.

The poetry Patrick wrote over the years, sentimental as it was, became a vehicle for expressing deep feelings. His love for his wife was intense as was his attachment to the five-year-old son who died and whose loss he memorialized in verse. Patrick was noticeably happy when he had his children with him, whether on Sunday outings to lower Manhattan or walks to Coney Island or for the family card games they enjoyed as adults.

Patrick's active Irish wit combined with his attachment to people to counteract and soften his sterner nature. The same humor with which he thanked LaGuardia in rhyme for his approval of vacation days was often in evidence. He had an Irish gift for seeing the amusing in daily human situations and would enrich the telling in his loud, rapid-fire brogue.

Patrick's lifestyle was genuinely simple as is often the case with immigrants. Friends at one time counseled him that with his two lawyer sons and his own broad contacts in New York City he was naturally equipped to launch a successful business venture. Patrick gave them a deadpan stare and replied in full brogue, "And what would I be doing with the money?" Material things did not appear to tempt him at all. He was fond of repeating the old adage, "We come into the world without anything and we leave it similarly." In an editorial in the fire department magazine, he wrote:

Material luxuries, while helpful, can never give a man true happiness or contentment. . . . Peace, happiness and content ment cannot be bought with money, and neither can fame, health or power. . . .[1]

If religion was the sun in Patrick's universe, then patriotism was its moon. Students of Irish history and of the Irish in America point to the tendency in this ethnic group to interweave, almost to identify, religion and patriotism. In the struggle for Catholic emancipation in Ireland, religion and nationalism had been united in a common cause. In the United States, the anti-Catholic tendencies in the dominant Protestant culture ironically served to strengthen for the Irish the link between religion and patriotism.[2] Although the parochial school separated Catholic young people from an environment hostile to their faith, it nevertheless emphasized patriotism and allegiance to the newly adopted country. Non-Catholics commonly accused the Catholic school system of undermining the public school's transmission of an American culture and this accusation only sharpened the determination of parochial schools to graduate youngsters as imbued with "Americanism" as their public school counterparts. In fact, the Catholic system seemed to believe it was more American. While public schools sought to disassociate from any religious context and distanced themselves at times from moral questions lest they infringe on their professed neutrality, Catholic authorities insisted they were instilling in their pupils the basic moral values of the country's founding fathers.

Patrick expressed this position in a speech he wrote and delivered to a gathering of the Knights of Columbus during World War II.

This Nation was founded on the belief in God. When the Founding Fathers wrote the Declaration of Independence, they, at the same time, wrote a declaration of dependence on God. . . .We must have not only a faith in God but we must also have a faith in our government, in our public officials and in our armed forces. With such faith we can have confidence in victory. . . .[3]

Irish-Americans, however, took their identification of religion and patriotism one step farther. If they saw themselvesasdefenders of basic American values and institutions, then it could follow, in their thinking, that an attack on Catholic values was an attack on America.[4]

Self-appointed guardians of the country's values, Catholics were among the first to be alarmed over the dangers of atheistic Communism. They regarded the Communist threat to religion as a challenge to the underpinnings of the American way of life. They thought of themselves as true Americans warning their countrymen of a serious threat to the American system.

In his attitude toward Communism, Patrick was typically Irish-American. In other significant ways as well his life reflected the Irish immigrant story in the late Nineteenth and early Twentieth Centuries. Although a number of Irish did make their way to the Midwestern farmlands, the majority settled in the urban areas of the Atlantic coast: New York, Philadelphia, Boston. By 1920, ninety percent of all Irish Americans resided in cities.[5] They strongly believed city employment was a step upward and large numbers entered the police and fire departments. The close ties between the Irish and urban politics ensured that this group would dominate the ranks of civil service in the northeastern cities for several decades. Besides their affinity for politics and civil service, the Irish had a penchant for careers in law and the church, the directions pursued by Patrick's children.

Patrick might have gone farther in his career than the majority of his immigrant countrymen but the path he pursued in civil service, his devotion to his church, his adherence to the Democratic party, the manner in which he raised his family were all decidedly in the mainstream of the Irish experience in America.

The story of a life can be told; the summing up of a person is difficult and elusive. Beneath the lofty ideals Patrick Walsh professed and sincerely sought to embody throughout his life, one looks for signs of an inner struggle, of the human wrestling with that part of the self that tends to resist the constant striving. Perhaps some indication can be found in a line of an editorial he wrote in July, 1945:

> It takes moral courage in its highest sense to stick to the path of a good and decent life.[6]

One may ask, What were his temptations along that path when he needed moral courage to pursue the good and decent life? At the start of his autobiography, Patrick had written that his true philosophy of life could be summed up in the words of the catechism: "God made me to know Him, to love Him and to serve Him in this world and to be happy with Him forever in the next." But he added the comment, "I only know too well how often I have forgotten it." Were these words echoes of the ritual lament of the humble Christian, or did Patrick mean something more personal?

In piecing together the pastiche of bits and pieces of information about the man's public and private life, one misses evidence to indicate that Patrick possessed any noticeable degree of psychological awareness. It cannot be ruled out since, for instance, no communications between husband and wife survive. But in the recollections of his son and those of relatives and friends of the family there is nothing to suggest that Patrick was sensitive to the psychological dimension of human life. His strong belief in "mind over matter" seemed to prevail. Perhaps one can conjecture that his feelings of having strayed from the path or of having forgotten his basic philosophy came from a sense of unworthiness over the darker urges that surface in any person, even those of the sharpest vigilance — perhaps especially in those.

Patrick's competitiveness and will to succeed was an example to his children that he believed needed no justification. Did it not go without saying that achievements, doing one's best, were goals for every human being? Weren't they basic to the notion of service to God, one's family and the public good? When Patrick took his oath of office as commissioner, he pledged to Mayor LaGuardia to do even better than his best. But there are indications he may have had additional motivation for his need to achieve, that there might have been a link between the approval of others, which came to him with success, and his own self-acceptance. How better to compensate for feelings of unworthiness than to hear others praising him, especially when those others were voices of authority, whether of the church or of the city bureaucracy. This particular motive for his ambition was probably hidden from him.

What were the circumstances that might have encouraged a sense of unworthiness in Patrick or left him uncertain about his own abilities? He seemed confident and very competitive as a farm boy in Ireland who wanted the latest machinery for reaping the biggest harvest. That urge was strong enough to provoke a break with his father. This being the case, his early experience in America must have come as a blow to the cocky youth.

He arrived in the "land of opportunity" to discover that jobs were difficult to find. His weeks of initial search were giving him a message he had not anticipated, that it would not be easy for an Irish farm boy to get ahead in the big city on a foreign continent. Determined to survive, he was thrown back on the farm work he thought he had put behind him, first five months on Staten Island and, following another unsuccessful job hunt, a three-year stay tending property in rural New Jersey. That extended experience could well have diminished Patrick's self-confidence.

Mary Ann's coming from Ireland to marry him strengthened Patrick for another attempt to establish himself in New York. Landing the position of a ferryman in late 1891 brought him hope and he settled with his wife into a household of his own. But the ferry job lasted five full years, and when it became clear there was no advancement in it for him, he turned to bartending for Tom Foley. There he spent five more years, under the increasing burden of a growing family. In addition to his lack of formal education, he must have encountered anti-Irish and anti-Catholic discrimination. Promotion in the Union Ferry Company had been denied him because he was not Protestant and a Mason. Adding to these deflating experiences was the fact his home was on the fringe of the stately Brooklyn Heights neighborhood where the Irish were the domestics, the maintenance and delivery men.

In sum, Patrick had spent thirteen and a half years in his adopted country and had nothing to show for it. He had not "made it" in the economic and social sense and the deaths of four of his children seriously depressed his spirits. It is understandable that he contemplated returning to Ireland to start a new life in a more kindly environment.

The opportunity to join the fire department in 1901 brought the new direction he had been seeking and ended any thought of returning home. The city bureaucracy was prestigious employment to the Irish immigrant and the fire department was a uniformed service tinged with danger and a touch of glamor. Best of all, there was room for advancement. For the first time in the new country he was at a point where he could compete and get ahead. After such a long experience of negative messages from his surroundings, Patrick must have longed for the chance to prove himself. Prove himself to himself, first of all — that seemed to be at the heart of the matter.

Perhaps the feelings of unworthiness Patrick alluded to toward the end of his life had roots in some awareness of his obsession with succeeding. Apparently he was not above using influence for getting ahead, if such were available. At the outset, Tom Foley of Tammany Hall was most likely his sponsor for entering the fire department. The pool of candidates for city jobs was so enormous, particularly for the "Irish-owned" fire and police departments, that connections were essential. But it must be said for Patrick that any help he received was an adjunct to his own talent. He consistently prepared himself for promotional examinations and did well on them. His early rise was swift. But in reviewing his overall career, there were long periods in which he remained stationary. Positions became fewer in number as a fireman climbed the ladder and competition for openings was necessarily keener. As battalion chief, his sights were on deputy chief, but seven years passed before his advancement.

Son Paul remembered his father's impatience at having to stand still in the same job. Paul, as a high school boy, occasionally accompanied his father to the Tammany Hall headquarters on Fourteenth

Street. As a loyal Democrat, his son attests, Patrick tried to drop in at the party center once a month. "He stayed in with the leaders just in case they could put in a good word for him," according to Paul.

Patrick's pride, his need to achieve, had earlier provoked the confrontation with his father in Ireland. His children believed that rift was never healed, that no reconciliation had taken place before the elder Patrick died in 1903 at age fifty-four. For someone so devoted to obedience and authority, it is hard to understand why Patrick never reached out to his father in later years. Perhaps as he matured, and had his father lived longer, it would have happened. The fact it never did is perhaps another clue to the son's sense of personal unworthiness. His pride might have been the source of his own admission that he had often forgotten that life was basically about loving and serving God.

Patrick's anxiety over achievement was part of the legacy he delivered to his children. One could accept oneself when others did so; outer confirmation was important. With reliance on principles and outside authority for guidance, there was little need to think for oneself in important matters. The result of such training had to be a thwarting of growth toward self-confidence and independence.

It is ironic Patrick's strong will worked in two directions. He had rebelled against his father but demanded total control of his own children. He could not afford to pass on the spirit of rebelliousness and, moreover, he was probably ashamed of it in the light of the duty of love and obedience toward parents. But he disliked what he had read in his father as weakness and resolved to make his children in his own determined mold. One searches in vain for evidence Patrick might have considered the merits of encouraging independence of character within his own family.

Mike and Joe had to go as far as possible in their own careers to gain their father's approval as well as their own. Michael became a State Supreme Court judge and Joseph general counsel for Sinclair Oil Company. On the other hand, Jack, Paul and Mary entered religious life where different criteria prevailed. The religious vocation was, in itself, the more perfect way — just by persevering in it they earned their father's approval. Jerry never won. The high point of his life that had made his father proud was his World War I adventures as a seaman. His failure to get anywhere in the years that followed visibly disappointed Patrick. There were not even children to show for the marriage. One can speculate if the years of Jerry's illness, with unspecific and changing diagnoses, and his premature death at forty-three had psychological underpinnings in his relationship with his father. There was a mellow quality in Jerry's personality that might possibly have reflected the Ryans on his mother's side, or perhaps — indeed — was a throwback to Patrick's father.

If Patrick never really understood the root causes of his need for achievement, it would follow that he was blind to anything negative in transmitting this value to his children. After all, what could be more Christian or more American than striving to achieve the best, and certainly one's children could only profit from that lesson.

Patrick Walsh was a man who did his best. That he might have done it for too long is illustrated in these remarks printed at the time of his death:

> One of the most colorful firefighters of this generation . . . despite his advancing age, failing sight and lapses of memory, he tenaciously worked long hours, six days a week, responded to fires which his rank very well did not demand, took no time off, checked up on attendance and punctuality of others and patrolled the 11th floor with the zeal of a sentry.[7]

He did not quite know how to say, "It is enough. I have done all I could."

Patrick's years in charge of the fire department coincided with those of World War II. Even had he not been the traditionalist that he was, had he been determined to reorganize and innovate, the larger constraints of the war would not have allowed the time or the resources to work such changes. The fire department of the early 1940's was, in effect, drafted into New York's civilian defense efforts. It was left to Patrick's successors to reevaluate and update.

Someone had asked the newly appointed Commissioner Walsh

in 1941, "Suppose you had your life to live over again — what would you do?"

> "I risk the answer," he replied. "There are many things that I have done that I would not do, but this I have done and would do again — be a fireman, even with horses, steel poles and $66 a month. It's a grand job."[8]

And it is very likely that Patrick would have repeated the same words as he was retired from the department at the close of 1945.

❦ ❦ ❦

The final prayers after the Requiem were over now. The church emptied and the relatives filled the long rows of cars lined up at the curb behind the hearse. As the cars moved slowly down the street, two hundred firemen reverently raised their arms in the last salute to their former chief. The band struck up a farewell piece, a favorite of Patrick's, "Annie Laurie."

As crowds thinned, a short, solitary figure emerged, moving along the sidewalk at the side of the cortege until it picked up speed. Followed only by a small group of children, Fiorello LaGuardia was saying good-bye to a friend.

Funeral procession for Patrick Walsh passes Engine 224, Hicks Street, Brooklyn.

Notes

CHAPTER ONE

1. 1990 Correspondence with Peter Meskell, author of *History of Boherlahan-Dualla* (Midleton, Co. Cork: Litho Press Co., 1987)
2. Irish football is closer to soccer than to American football. Points are scored by kicking or punching a round ball over the goal or into the net. Players cannot throw the ball but may dribble, kick, punt, or punch it.
3. Robert Kee, The Green Flag (New York: Delacorte Press, 1972), p. 426.

CHAPTER TWO

1. Robert Lewis Taylor, "Profiles," *The New Yorker,* April 25, 1942, p.21.
2. Robert Stern, Gregory Gilmartin, John Masenguli, *New York 1900 (Metropolitan Architecture and Urbanism, 1890-1915),* (New York: Rizzoli, 1983), p. 145.
3. David McCullough, *The Great Bridge* (New York: Simon and Schuster, 1972), p. 105. Copyright 1972 by David McCullough. Reprinted by permission of Simon and Schuster.
4. McCullough, p. 545.
5. McCullough, p. 111.
6. McCullough, p. 104
7. 1890 estimates place the population of New York City who were Irish born or of Irish parents at 27.5%. As reported in Florence E. Gibson, *The Attitudes of the New York Irish towards State and National Affairs 1848-1892,* (New York: Columbia University Press, 1951), p. 428.
8. Tammany Hall was the best known of the political machines the two-party system had produced in America. The Irish vote counted heavily in New York City through the last half of the 19th and first few decades of the 20th centuries and Tammany was an efficient instrument for turning out that vote on election day.

CHAPTER THREE

1. Stephen Phillips, "The Fireman."
2. Patrick Walsh, "My Johnny Days," *WNYF*, October, 1941,   Vol. 2, No. 4, p. 4.
3. John V. Morris, *Fires and Firefighters* (Boston: Little Brown & Co. 1953), p. 300.
4. Walsh, p. 4.
5. Lowell Limpus, *History of the New York City Fire Department* (New York: E.P. Dutton, 1940), p. 301.
6. *WNYF*, April 1945, Vol. 6, No. 2, p. 20.
7. Morris, pp. 302-303.
8. Morris, p. 356.
9. Dennis Smith, *Steely Blue* (New York: Simon & Schuster, 1984), pp. 96-98. Copyright 1984 by Dennis Smith. Reprinted by permission of Simon and Shuster.
10. As reported by Limpus, p. 289.

CHAPTER FOUR

1 "Fire Lines," an unidentified N.Y. Fire Department column published in 1936.
2. The N.Y. C. Fire Department Museum was moved to new quarters at 278 Spring Street, as of January, 1991.
3. *WNYF*, January 1942, Vol. 2, No. 1, p. 14.

CHAPTER SIX

1. New York *World Telegram*, June 12, 1936.

CHAPTER SEVEN

1. *WNYF*, "Division of Fire Prevention at Work," October 1941, Vol. 1, No. 4, pp. 5-7.

CHAPTER NINE

1. Richard Cox, "Coney Island: The Amusement Park as Urban Symbol in American Art," *Brooklyn: USA* (New York, Brooklyn College Press, 1979), p. 137-141.
2. *New York Times,* September 22, 1946.

CHAPTER TEN

1. "Scrapbook" No. 42, p. 59. This is one of a series of almost fifty volumes of a personal collection of newspaper and magazine articles belonging to the deceased Honorary Assistant Chief Clarence E. Meek whose collection of books and assorted other materials became, in 1938, the kernel of New York City Fire Department Library. A number of the newspaper articles and columns contained in the "Scrapbooks" are not identified as to source.

CHAPTER ELEVEN

1. Robert A. Caro, *The Power Broker* (New York: Vintage Books, 1975), p. 444.
2. Caro, p. 444-445.
3. Charles Garrett, *The LaGuardia Years: Machine and Reform Politics* in New York City (New Brunswick, N.J.: Rutgers University Press, 1961), p. 59.
4 William Manners, *Patience and Fortitude: Fiorello LaGuardia* (New York: Harcourt, Brace, Jovanovich, 1976), p. 3.
5. Garrett, p. 133.
6. Caro, p. 445.
7. Caro, p. 445.
8. Manners, p. 254.
9. "Scrapbook" No. 38, p. 52.
10. *New York Times,* May 11, 1941, p. 1.
11 *New York Times,* May 11, 1941, p. 1.
12 "Scrapbook" No. 36, p. 90.
13 "Scrapbook" No. 36, p. 101. (An unidentified New York City newspaper.)
14. Manners, p. 261.
15. Municipal Archives, LaGuardia Papers, mimeographed text of a speech June 27, 1944.

16. Taylor, *The New Yorker* (April 25, 1942), p. 28.
17. Municipal Archives, LaGuardia Papers, speech of June 27, 1944.
18. Taylor, p. 21.
19. Scrapbook" No. 37 (1941), p. 41; *The Chief* (July 5, 1941).
20. "Accent on Auxiliaries," *WNYF,* January 1942, Vol. 3, No. 1.
21. Jerry Daly, "New York Starts School for Training Auxiliaries," *Fire Engineering,* 1941 ("Scrapbook" No. 37, p. 30).
22. Taylor, p. 28.
23. "Scrapbook" No. 37, p. 37.
24. "Scrapbook" No. 37, p. 37.
25. *New York Times,* May 13, 1942.
26. La Guardia Archives, May 15, 1942.
27. LaGuardia Archives, memo to the mayor from Patrick Walsh, June 22, 1944.
28. LaGuardia Archives, Walsh memo of June 22, 1944.
29. Harvey Ardman, *Normandie, Her Life and Times* (New York: Franklin Watts, 1985).
30. Manners, p. 271.

CHAPTER TWELVE

1. Manners, p. 7.
2. Manners, p. 8.
3 LaGuardia Archives, PW to FHL, September 13, 1943.
4. LaGuardia Archives, October 8, 1944.
5. LaGuardia Archives, May 8, 1942.
6. LaGuardia Archives, September, 1942.
7. LaGuardia Archives, October 27, 1942.
8. LaGuardia Archives, January 6, 1943.
9. LaGuardia Archives, June 3, 1943.
10. LaGuardia Archives, June 3, 1943.
11. Taylor, p. 22.

CHAPTER THIRTEEN

1 *WNYF,* January 1943.
2. Speech at the Fire Department Holy Name Communion Breakfast, as reported in the *New York Times,* April 13, 1942.
3 "Scrapbook" No. 38, p. 120 (1942).
4 *New York Times,* April 1, 1943.

5   *New York Times*, April 1, 1943.
6   *New York Times*, December 31, 1943.
7. "Scrapbook" No. 36, p. 100, "Fire Chief" column (1941)
8   *New York Times*, January 27, 1944.
9. *New York Times*, January 27, 1944.
10. *Civil Service Leader*, June 6, 1944, p. 3.
11. *Civil Service Leader,*, June 6, 1944, p. 3.
12. *Civil Service Leader,*, July 25, 1944, p. 3.
13 *The New York Times*, June 21, 1944.
14 *The New York Times*, July 22, 1944.
15. *The New York Times*, July 4, 1944.
16. Francis Kelly, "The Real Facts Behind the LaGuardia/Fireman Feud," *Civil Service Leader*, January 18, 1944, p. 5.
17. *WNYF*, July 1941, Vol. 2, No. 3, p. 4.
18. "Scrapbook" No. 36 (1941), pp. 86, 90.
19. *WNYF,*, January 1943, Editorial, Vol. 4, No. 1,
20. "Scrapbook" No. 39 (1942), p. 41.
21. *F.D. Annual Report*, 1940, "The Commissioner's Message," p. 11.
22. *New York Times*, June 28, 1943.
23. LaGuardia speech at the annual memorial ceremony for firemen at Riverside Drive monument.
24. Emma Schweppe, *The Firemen's and Patrolmen's Unions in the City of New York* (New York: Kings Crown Press, Columbia University, 1948), p. 242.
25 *WNYF*, Vol. 7, No. 1, p. 3.
26. *WNYF*, Vol. 2, No. 4 (1941), p. 4.

CHAPTER FOURTEEN

1   *New York Times*, July 29, 1945, p. 1; Charles F. Haywood, *General Alarm* (New York: Dodd, Mead & Co., 1967), pp. 197-198; Gerhart E. Bryant and Arthur J. Golden, "Empire Crash Fire," *WNYF*, October 1945, vol. 6, No. 4, pp. 4-7.
2. *New York Times*, April 9, 1945.
3. *New York Times*, August 23, 1945, p. 25.
4. Manners, p. 265.
5. *New York Times*, August 11, 1945.
6. *New York Times*, November 19, 1945.
7. Manners, p. 267.
8. *New York Times*, September 21, 1947 (Manners, p. 277).

CHAPTER FIFTEEN

1. *WNYF*, January 1945, Vol. 6, No. 1, p. 3.
2. See especially Jay P. Dolan, *The Immigrant Church (New York's Irish & German Catholics 1815-1865)* (Baltimore: Johns Hopkins University Press, 1975), p. 54.
3. From a mimeographed text, May 1942.
4. R.H. Bayor, *Neighbors in Conflict, The Irish, German, Jews and Italians in New York City, 1929-1941* (Baltimore: Johns Hopkins University Press, 1978), p. 92.
5. *Harvard Encyclopedia of American Ethnic Groups*, Stephen Thernstrom, Ed., (Cambridge, MA: Belknap Press of Harvard University Press, 1980), p. 530.
6. *WNYF*, Vol. 6, No. 3, p. 3.
7. "Scrapbook" No. 43 (1946), p. 44, from *The Chief.*
8. *WNYF*, October 1941, Vol. 2, No. 4, p. 4.

Other Books in the
Fire Service History Series
from Fire Buff House Publishers

- **Chemical Fire Engines** *by W. Fred Conway*
  The only book ever written about the amazing engines that for 50 years (1872 to 1922) put out 80% of all fires in the United States.

- **Fire Boats** *by Paul Ditzel*
  The definitive book on the history of marine firefighting by the "Dean of Fire Authors."

- **A Century of Service** *by Paul Ditzel*
  The official history of the City of Los Angeles Fire Department, the second largest fire department in the world.

- **Fire Alarm!** *by Paul Ditzel*
  The fascinating story behind the red box on the corner. A history of fire alarm telegraphy with emphasis on Gamewell.

- **A Fire Chief Remembers** *by Chief Edwin B. Schneider (Ret.) F.D.N.Y.*
  The poignant, touching, moving account of his fascinating career during the 1930's, 40's and 50's. Chief Schneider writes from his heart.

- **Visiting America's Fire Museums** *by W. Fred Conway*
  The first and only comprehensive illustrated directory of over 175 museums in America displaying vintage fire apparatus and memorabilia.

Fire Buff House Publishers
P.O. Box 711, New Albany, Indiana 47151
Phone 1-800-457-2400